Ladies of Letters . . . and More

D1396447

Also available

Ladies of Letters
More Ladies of Letters
Ladies of Letters.com
Ladies of Letters Log On

BBC Worldwide audio titles

Ladies of Letters . . . and More
Ladies of Letters.com
Ladies of Letters Log On

Ladies of Letters ... and More

The Early Works of
Vera Small and Irene Spencer

Carole Hayman and Lou Wakefield

GRANADA

Ladies of Letters was first published in
Great Britain in 1991 and by Granada Media in 2000
More Ladies of Letters was first published in
Great Britain in 2000 by Granada Media
This edition first published in Great Britain in 2001
by Granada Media, an imprint of André Deutsch Limited
20 Mortimer Street
London W1V 5HA

In association with Granada Media Group

A catalogue record for this title is available from the British Library

ISBN 0 233 99986 8

Cover illustration by Sarah Perkins
Cover design by Matthew Bookman at BBC Worldwide

Typeset by
Derek Doyle & Associates, Liverpool.
Printed in the UK by
Mackays of Chatham PLC.

10 9 8 7 6 5 4 3 2 1

The audio titles *Ladies of Letters . . . and More* and *Ladies of Letters.com*
are both BBC Radio Collection Worldwide titles

Contents

Ladies of Letters   1
More Ladies of Letters   155

Ladies of Letters

Foreword

Casa Richa
Marbella
Espanol

Knowing my interest in collecting historical documents, my friends Lou Wakefield and Carole Hayman passed me a bundle of letters after finding them in the drawer of a melamine bedside cabinet (which was being offered for sale at a car boot sale in Walmer, Kent). The correspondence is between a Mrs Spencer and a Mrs Small.

I have spent many a night with those important letters spread out in front of me. How homesick I felt for England.

What fascinating glimpses of lower-middle-class life they afford. How Irene Spencer and Vera suffered for their families. Medals should be struck in their honour.

Irene is a 'plain cook' and Vera an 'exotic', which says it all perhaps. But, despite these differences, a friendship grows and a relationship develops. These unknown women (sadly neither is now to be found at the same address, and the Salvation Army has drawn a blank), these bastions of English society, have unknowingly presented us with an accurate social document. Clippings from the local press provide welcome background material. Thanks to Vera and Irene, future generations will be able to read this book and know what it was like to live in the late 1980s. Social historians wishing to know what a 'knitted thermal boob tube' is will turn to this book in gratitude.

The letters are indeed fascinating on matters domestic (the book is awash with household hints and recipes), but broad social issues are not neglected. Irene writes to Vera from Grossthorpe police cells after her arrest for contravening the Public Order Act and events take a dramatic turn when both ladies are subsequently imprisoned aboard HM Prison Ship *Pride of Cleveland*. But typically, they manage to maintain their correspondence by the ingenious use of prison-issue toilet paper. Others are drawn into the correspondence. Vera's son, Howard, a somewhat regressive type, writes to his mother on organic brown rice paper informing her that he is suffering from alopecia. Karen, Vera's daughter, is in permanent crisis, and Bruce, a Church of England clergyman, writes from the vicarage on both sides of a communion wafer. But it is Irene, released on the grounds of insanity, who battles for her friend Vera's freedom, organising a 'Vera Small's Innocent', Fork and Finger Buffet.

These letters will appeal to anyone who is on a rota to arrange church flowers, those interested in penal reform, and students of family life. I found them to be quite compelling. Quite honestly as I laid the last letter aside I felt a better person for having glimpsed behind the net curtains of Mrs Small and Mrs Spencer's turbulent lives.

Since writing the above foreword my circumstances have changed. I no longer live at my villa Casa Rich, I prefer a more cloistered academic atmosphere. I have Mrs Spencer and Mrs Small to thank for this change of direction in my life. I am now Professor Emeritus at Marbella University and am sponsored by the Spencer/Small Foundation to promote the need for retaining the existence of older women. My course is called 'The uses of older women – an exploration' (all enquiry's about course fees to the above address).

I know them so well through their letters, yet it remains my fervent hope to meet Mrs Small and Mrs Spencer in the flesh, one day.

Sue Townsend
2000

34 Wormwold Way
Hethergreen

14 July

Dear Vera,

Thank you for your 'thank-you' letter of the 9th – yes, it was a lovely day. I had a postcard from Lesley and Keith this morning from Lanzarote: food superb, weather glorious, gorgeous hotel – I shall pop round to the new house tomorrow to order the milk and papers.

It was kind of you to write a thank-you note. So few people bother now – you'd be surprised, out of a hundred guests and thirty-five others who were posted cake, how many just don't seem to think. I did enjoy your company at the reception and am much obliged for the loan of your handkerchief (laundered and returned, enclosed). It seems a shame you live so far away, since we seem to share so many of the same interests. Perhaps we'll become pen-pals instead!

Must close as Sidney is howling for his tea. The house seems so empty now, I'm glad of his company, so he's getting a bit spoilt I'm afraid.

The secret of my taramasalata dip is that I mix the roe with cottage cheese, and perhaps a *few* breadcrumbs, so that it is not too oily. It always proves popular at parties.

Kind regards,

Irene Spencer

The Gables
Little Potterton

16 July

Dear Irene,

Thank you so much for your note thanking me for my
'thank-you' letter. I quite agree that not enough people
bother these days. Courtesy costs nothing, I always say
(unless you count the cost of the stamp! Isn't it an awful
price!). I felt quite down when I returned home. I do love
an 'occasion' and now my children are both so far away I
don't often get them. In fact the last was Gerald's funeral.
Still, I mustn't complain.

You will miss Lesley at first, I am sure. She is a lovely
girl and looked quite magical in her wedding gown. Ivory
taffeta has always been a favourite of mine – I was so glad
when Princess Diana decided on it. Still, Keith seems a
pleasant chap. I tried your taramasalata on the vicar's wife
and she said she'd never tasted anything like it. Exchange
is no robbery, so here is one of my stand-bys.

Crumble a packet of digestive biscuits into a pan of
bittersweet melted chocolate and butter. Mix well. Turn
into a flat pie dish and press well down. Pop into the
freezer. Delicious as a teatime snack or cut into squares as
petits fours. Gerald always had a very sweet tooth.

Well, I must close now as it is time for *A Book at Bedtime*.
It's the *Boston Strangler* this week. Do let's keep in touch. I
love to get a letter in the morning. It makes the day, I feel.
Of course the children write – when they can.

All the best,

Vera

34 Wormwold Way
Hethergreen

21 July

Dear Vera,

Your letter has thrown me into utter mental turmoil
and I haven't slept a wink since receiving it. I've not
been able to settle to anything, and finally I thought,
well, you'll just have to face her with it, so that is what I
am doing. After all, honesty's the best policy, and if in
doubt, say you don't know.

Now, I'm going to say some things in total confidence,
and I'll hope that it will go no further. I should hate
everybody to think I was a fool, even if I am. It's so very
embarrassing, I don't know how to put it. Of course you
know that I had a hundred guests to invite. Well, Lesley
and Keith wrote out a list, and Keith's parents, and I
added mine to it, so I lost track a bit of who was who.
Things are such a burden when you're on your own (as
of course you know) – there's so much to keep in your
mind. Still, no excuses, fair's fair. The long and the short
of it is, I thought you were one of Keith's family when I
met you. It wasn't until in your last letter you said,
'Lesley is a lovely girl . . . Keith seems a pleasant chap',
that I had the inkling of an idea that you weren't one of
his aunties. I could have sworn that's what somebody
said at the reception. Are you perhaps one of Lesley's
old teachers, or a friend from where she used to work? I
know she had some coming. Please don't say you are
one of my family, or I think I shall go quite mad. Perhaps
I am already. I do forget people's names now I'm older,
and I mislay things constantly.

Proof of the pudding: I just made myself a cup of
Ovaltine after that last sentence, and then I couldn't find

my pen. I searched high and low. Finally I found it behind my ear. I *never* put a pen behind my ear, I don't think. You see, I feel now that I can't be sure of anything any more. I've really come to mistrust myself. This is how old ladies are supposed to go, isn't it? But I'm only sixty-two. I dare hardly go to the shops any more, in case I walk out and forget to pay, like Lady Barnett used to – and look what happened to her!

Now, I hope this won't spoil our friendship, because I did so enjoy your company. I've certainly not danced a tango like that in years – before I was married in fact. And this brings me to my second point. I do remember that we enjoyed a quantity of liquid libation, and in the heat of the moment I might have broken the rule of a lifetime and uttered one or two confidences to you. I shan't say what they were, in case I didn't. There are a couple of small things of a personal nature that I'd rather not tell the world and his wife, if you know what I mean, and if I did tell you, then please, please, forget them.

Oh dear, all this sounds very dramatic, doesn't it? I'm not usually an emotional person, I can assure you. Perhaps it's the shock of Lesley and Keith deciding to stay a week longer. I've had to go and cancel the milk and papers and turn everything off, and of course the newsagent looked at me as if I were a perfect fool. If they'd come home as planned, I could have asked Lesley who you were, but then again perhaps I wouldn't have. Children get so irritable when you forget things, don't they?

Please forgive this outburst. I'm sure it's all a simple misunderstanding.

With sincerest good wishes,

Irene

PS I've been too depressed to make up your recipe yet, but it sounds delicious.

30 July

My dear Irene,

Sorry to have been a while answering your letter. The postman (silly fool) unfortunately delivered it to the wrong 'Gables' – the one in *Great* Potterton – and Mrs Wavertree was two days bringing it round (she finds it hard to get out with her arthritic knee). Then she delivered it when I was out and the dog hid it in her basket. I discovered it, partly chewed, when I gave her blanket a good shake this morning.

I was upset to think you have been on tenterhooks waiting for my answer. I *do* know what you mean about this absent-minded business. Only yesterday I set off to the shop for toilet paper and came back with a tin of Cherry Blossom and twenty cigarettes. I wouldn't mind, but I haven't smoked since I was twelve! Sometimes I think I would forget my own name if it wasn't on a chain round my neck. Karen gave it to me for my last birthday and I wonder if it wasn't a hint.

To put your mind at rest, no, we have never met before, and I'm not really from either 'side'. I'm an old friend of Betty's and as I was staying with her when she 'masterminded' your catering, I thought I might as well give her a hand. The salmon mousse and the blue cheese quiche were mine. Betty and I used to do 'functions' together before I moved. More a hobby than anything really.

I *do* recall having one or two sherries, but I've no memory at all of dancing the tango. Are you sure it was me? Gerald always used to say I had two left feet, though I was considered quite a jitterbugger in my youth. As to any confidences, I can assure you they are quite safe with me. Betty says I passed out as soon as I got in the car, and the next morning I left as soon as I had drunk a black coffee. I would have liked to have lingered, but Mabel Thrush (my next-door neighbour) would only look after the dog until Sunday.

It's nice to think that you felt you could confide in me though, on so short an acquaintance. I've often longed for a friend to talk to about 'personal' matters. Men don't encourage intimacy do they? I always felt rather a hysterical fool if I got 'emotional' about anything with Gerald. How have you filled your extra week without Lesley and Keith? Pity I didn't know sooner or you could have popped up here for a couple of days . . . Must stop now as Mabel is at the door. I expect she's 'on the borrow' again. Take care of yourself and steer clear of the sherry bottle!

All the best,

Vera

2 August

Dear Vera,

Thank you for your letter, albeit tardy. Lesley and Keith are back from Lanzarote now, and it's nice to have things back to normal. I apologise for my letter. I have been under the doctor recently but am better now thanks to the tablets.

I don't know quite what you mean by your parting remark about staying away from the sherry bottle. Tippling has never been a vice I have fallen foul of, and sherry has never been my drink. If you are gaining your impressions from the reception, I can assure you that that was the exception that proves the rule, and if a mother can't get tipsy at her only daughter's wedding, I don't know what to think.

Thank you for your offer to stay with you, albeit in retrospect, but I should have had to refuse. I can't leave Sidney on his own, and Lesley is the only one besides me that he can tolerate, and who know his habits.

I have tried your recipe, but I found it rather rich.

Yours sincerely,

Irene Spencer

The Gables

10 August

Dear Irene,

Just a note to let you know I've had a little spell in hospital since I last wrote. Sorry it's so short but I've still got my arm in a sling. The fact is that I had a silly fall the very morning your letter arrived! I was running upstairs to get my writing paper and the dog (she's forever under my feet) had parked herself right at the top. I don't know why – perhaps I was in a bit of a state – but I just didn't see her and down I went. I've had concussion, cracked ribs and a nasty sprained wrist.

Hope you are keeping well.

Yours,

Vera

12 August

Dear Vera,

Words cannot express the shame and remorse I feel at having caused you such misery. Are you very poorly? Of course you are, what a stupid question! I remember only too well when I sprained my ankle on the garage door, to conjure up visions of black swelling and agony. It is one of those swing-up-and-over affairs, and Clive was in such a hurry to watch the cricket and was hooting at me to make haste. Somehow my slacks had got caught up in the mechanism, and as I threw the door upwards, I suddenly found myself hanging upside down, suspended by one leg. The pain when I came round was excruciating (the doctor said I'd been lucky to escape a fracture), and I was too much in physical distress to see the humorous side of it, which Clive certainly did as he helped me down. Afterwards at dinner parties, he used to joke that seeing me like that almost made up for missing Botham make the winning century.

I feel so culpable (is that the right word?) for making you fall. If I hadn't written that rather starchy letter, you wouldn't have been running upstairs at all. Lesley's yoga teacher says that negative energy is bound to beget negative results, and I must say now that I've had proof positive. I am going to buy one of those ionizers to see if that will charge the atmosphere at home in a more constructive way, and also between you and me, I'm going to stop taking the tablets the doctor prescribed – they make me feel so depressed.

I hope you are enjoying the flowers I sent – I asked for a mixture of yellow – always such a cheering colour I feel – so I hope they followed my instructions. The girl at the florist's *looked* as if she'd understood me, but you never can tell.

Incidentally, just to put the record straight, I did enjoy your chocolate square recipe. I said it was rich because I was angry, but in actual fact I gorged the whole lot myself the evening that Lesley and Keith returned from their honeymoon, so I've only got myself to blame for being sick afterwards.

I do hope you're feeling a little bit better now, and look forward to hearing from you.

With kindest regards for a speedy recovery,

Irene

27 August

Dear Irene,

Thank you for the kind letter. You are a silly to think
that I blame you in any way for the fall. I'm sure I never
intended to give that impression and I feel terrible that
you have been lacerating yourself about it. The flowers
were lovely by the way, sweet peas in pink and mauve – I
always think they are so uretheal-looking, though of
course they don't last. Mabel had to clear them out by the
time I returned from my few days away. Did you get my
PC? Mabel didn't receive hers until two days after I was
back. You might as well send stuff by carrier pigeon!

In case you didn't, an old friend of mine, Audrey
Roscoe, runs a little guest house nearby on the coast, and I
popped off there for a few days' recuperation. I must say I
was made a fuss of. Audrey is a great one for chat – in fact
most nights my head was ringing by the time we got to
bed, and on the Tuesday I went down with an awful
migraine – but all the cooking was done by hand, and the
views from her bay window are quite panamaric. Of course
it rained like a drain the whole time, but I just put on my
old boots and waterproof jerkin and strode off across the
pebbles. I don't care what anyone says, sea air does make
you feel better – you should try it. Nothing drives the
'blues' away quicker than a brisk walk in a howling gale. I
was quite sorry to have to come back and pick up the
'threads' again. Mabel had got me in one or two provisions,
which was very kind, although she will buy that long-life
milk and she knows I can't stand it. But you should have
seen the pile of bills (Gerald always used to call it 'hate'
mail) awaiting my return! Also a tile had come off the roof
and water had poured into the attic on to my old sewing
machine, which I believe is quite a collector's item these
days. Sometimes you wonder if it's worth it!

How are Lesley and Keith? You hardly mention them in your last. Any holiday snaps? I'd love to see them and the wedding ones if it isn't too much bother. I found a couple of petals in the pocket of that two-piece I wore. I believe they are off your hat! Do you want them back? They are rather crumpled, I'm afraid!

Best regards,

Vera

Irene Spencer

34 Wormwold Way

Hethergreen

Dear Irene,

Having a few blowy days down by the sea. Hobbled as far as the front for these p.c.'s but I'm all done in after a few yards. Could hardly make it to the ladies conveniences — now I know how the dog feels! Audrey has just tacked me up with Jack the Ripper and a steaming hot mug of Bovril.

Best Wishes,
Vera

'Spumy Sea', photo by Craig Douglas.

28 August

Dear Vera,

I am glad to hear you have had a rest and are on the road to recovery, and *what* a coincidence that you know Audrey Roscoe. I knew her some long time ago before she moved to the coast, and never quite took to her. You are absolutely right when you say she's a chatterer – mostly rather catty gossip unfounded on fact, I seem to remember. Although I'm sure she wouldn't remember me.

Don't bother returning the petals – I shall never use that hat again as a hat. I shall snip the remaining blooms off and use them as the central theme for my Yuletide table decoration. It'll be nice to remember the wedding at Christmas. Lesley should be about ready for some home cooking then! I've hardly seen them since they've been back – they must be so busy settling in. Of course she doesn't want my help; she has to do everything by herself. Oh well, I suppose I was the same when I was first married, until I learned that a mother really *is* a girl's best friend. Unfortunately my own mother passed away shortly after I'd learned to appreciate her, a tragedy that I have regretted bitterly ever since.

Well, cheerio for now, I shall have to get on. I've got to pop into the village to get one or two essentials, and I shall go into the florist while I'm down there and give her a piece of my mind. That's the second time she's got the order wrong and it just isn't good enough. She made my memorial tribute to Clive a sheaf instead of a wreath, and I'd expressly said in the *Chronicle* 'no cut flowers'. I'm sure his sister Doreen still thinks it was done on purpose to draw attention to myself.

The postman's just delivered your postcard. I've never cared much for that part of the country – it's so flat and insipid, isn't it? What a shame the weather was so dreadful! Still, a change is as good as a rest. Take care of yourself and don't overdo things.

Kind regards,

Irene

10 September

Dear Irene,

I've been so busy since I got back, what with the garden – the lawn was full of moss – and the bottling season, that it's a pleasure to have only to sit down and write a letter. I am looking out on to a glorious sunset (one of the best features of a picture window) and a haze of blue smoke. At first I thought the house was on fire, but then I realised they were just burning the stubble in the neighbouring fields. This part of the country is so picturesque in the autumn. I have been jamming and pickling like a lunatic. Six pounds of gooseberry, four of bramble jelly, three of greengage, and some pear and walnut chutney. I love an oriental recipe. Really, it is silly to do so much – last year's is still in the larder – but it's such a hard habit to break, isn't it, doing things for a *family*?

I am hoping Karen will come for Christmas so she can take some back. Actually I'm a bit worried about her. She's gone terribly faddy with her food, won't eat meat and goes berserk about chemical additives. I hope she doesn't count pectin, or I shall have to take the lot to the Bring and Buy! Howard never notices what he's eating – just like a man! so he's easy to please. Must close now. Mabel Thrush has been rather poorly and the vicar is going to pop in shortly. She got in an awful fluster about him seeing the state of the place (she's a bit of a fanatic for the Hoover), so I have had to clean all her brass and make a Battenburg for tea.

Yours in haste,

Vera

PS I'm so glad the card arrived. I was afraid the GPO would make me out a liar. Fancy you knowing Audrey!

She did mention you as a matter of fact, but I always take everything she says with a pinch of salt.

3 October

Dear Irene,

I have been in such a state since I last wrote that it has taken me all this time to realise I have not had a reply to my last. I am so worried. Are you ill, or has some kind of crisis occurred? Do put me out of my anxiety with a note however brief. I am up to my eyes in plaster dust and rubble. I feel rather like a victim of the Mexico City earthquake. The builders are in. They came to replace a tile in the roof, but one of them put his foot through the ceiling and brought the lot down. They had to take up the carpet, and then discovered some beetle in a floorboard. Too late I discovered I am allergic to woodworm spray, and am now attending outpatients for chronic asthma and staying with Mabel Thrush. Write to me at home – I pop in once a day to collect the mail and wrench a few more artyfacts out of the debris.

Yours affec.,

Vera

7 October

Dear Vera,

I'm so sorry not to have corresponded before now and to get you into a tizz. I am absolutely fine, thank you, so there is no cause for concern. I do hope you are more organised with the builders now. Personally I always pay that little bit extra and get a reputable firm. It saves time and money in the long run.

To be quite frank, I didn't write at first because of my annoyance over Audrey Roscoe. I bet I know what she said about me, and it has very little basis in truth. Clive was very drunk at the time, and didn't know what he was doing, and anyway I was on holiday. But I don't know why I'm bothering to go into it. It's all in the past and that sort of woman isn't worth the paper and ink.

Anyway, that isn't the main reason why I didn't write, only the first reason, which I soon got over, and am completely over now. In fact if you see her again, do please give her my kindest regards, and tell her I hope her son is better now. He went to prison, you know – did she tell you? I think that's why she moved so far away.

I can't write much more just now, because Bill is coming over to take me out to a dinner dance. Life has been so hectic since he has been paying his attentions, and I must say it has perked me up no end. He is a widower, and an old friend of Clive's and mine. His wife died very slowly and painfully last year, and I have never seen a man so devoted. Actually he was at Lesley's wedding. You may remember him. He wore a grey morning suit, where most of the men wore tails. I'm sure you'd like him very much. He is what used to be called a gentleman.

Actually, most Sundays we go out for a run in his car, and I have been thinking of suggesting that we drive over to see you. It's just a suggestion of course, and I quite understand if you're too busy. Bill says he knows an exquisite French restaurant quite near Little Potterton – he knows the owners very well – and he says he would be delighted to take us both there for Sunday lunch. Would you enjoy that? Life can be so lonely on your own, I know. Anyway, I'll leave it with you and wait until you get in touch, but the first and third Sundays in November would be fine with us.

Do take care of your asthma. There's nothing worse than a nasty chest.

Fondest wishes,

Irene

20 October

Dear Irene,

How pleasant to hear from you at last. I am so glad you haven't allowed your new 'interest' to completely take over your life. I always think people live to regret abandoning old friends when new ones appear – particularly as one can never be certain how long these things will last. I do indeed remember 'Bill' from the reception. He was the one who dropped the salmon mousse all down his front, wasn't be? I remember he swore rather loudly – I assumed because his suit was hired. How nice that he has a car to take you around in. You know, you really should have learned to drive, there is no substitute for independent wheels. The times I have driven off and left Gerald pissed as a fart at some Round Table do or other!

Do by all means come over and see me one Sunday, though I can't recommend the restaurant you mention. It's called Les Liaisons Dangereuses and I must say their menu bears the name out. I certainly wouldn't put a strawberry Pernod sauce with halibut!

However, if you would like to sample some less reshershe dishes at my humble abode, I'd be delighted. It would have to be the third Sunday as the first is the Blood Donors' Remembrance Service, and I always do the flowers.

Best wishes,

Vera

PS My chest is much better. Mabel Thrush knitted me a thermal boob tube.

29 November

Dear Vera,

Just a little 'thank-you' note for such a pleasant day! It was lovely to see you after all this writing – you looked quite different to how I remembered, although of course you were just the same as your letters.

The lunch was superb! I've always admired people who cook in an exotic way. Personally I am a plain cook, but then so many men say that is what they like, don't they? I know Clive did. Anyway, Bill thought it was absolutely gorgeous, and on a par with Les Liaisons Dangerous.

I was so pleased that the two of you got on. It's so nice when one's friends like each other, isn't it? He thought you were lovely, very attractive. He's not stopped going on about how nice you looked in that two-piece you had on from Marks. He wanted me to buy one, but I think that style would drown me, don't you? When you're slim and fine-boned, you have to be very careful what you wear.

I'm so pleased to have seen your 'cottage' – how quaint! Now I can imagine you in your setting when I write.

What are you doing at Christmas? Is Karen coming home? I'm still hoping that Lesley and Keith will come here, but they still haven't committed themselves. Still, I dare say Bill will want to see me over the holidays, so it may be just as well if they don't come.

Anyway, must close, I'm running out of space on the notelet. Thank you once again for the lovely day. Bill said he would be writing to you himself, but I'll thank you from us both anyway. You know what men are like! You must come here soon.

Fond regards,

Irene

10 December

Dearest Irene,

Forgive me for being a while in answering. It has been all go here since Mabel Thrush went into hospital. Did I mention that she had to have her leg off? I have just come back from visiting now. She had run out of two-ply heliotrope and lemon barley water. I said to myself, that puts paid to her having the dog again, she'll never be able to take it 'walkies'. Some people will go to any lengths to avoid being neighbourly!

Talking of the dog, I do apologise for her behaviour when you visited – she really doesn't usually make that awful 'pong'. She gets nervous when strangers are in the house. As for her trying to climb on to Bill's lap – well! I had to laugh afterwards when I thought of the two of them struggling with the seat belt! Did you have a good journey back? I thought Bill was a trifle 'one over the eight'! He's written me a very nice note as a matter of fact. Funnily enough he's going to be in this area over the break, visiting some relations – do you know them? Perhaps he will bring you with him and we can all meet up for a glass of Christmas cheer. I must say I am at a loss over Christmas – Karen still hasn't said a word – I suppose it will depend upon the state of her 'relationship'. Howard is going to walk the Pennine Way with a friend. Seems a peculiar way to spend Christmas to me. I don't know whether to get food in or not. I suppose I will have to have Mabel in for Boxing Day, but frankly I'm not getting a huge bird just for me and her and the dog. I shall just depend on my deep-freeze.

I suppose you will be 'gadding' with Bill when the holiday season starts. How lovely to have some reasons for dressing up. I haven't worn my diamanté since the night Gerald died. By the way, I *loved* that tweed suit you were wearing. So comfy-looking and warm. Would you call that colour Biscuit? Don't take any notice of Bill – you've got your own taste and style, most definitely.

I'm off to do some Christmas shopping now so I will close. Do drop me a line before the awful whirl takes over. I don't know about you, but the sight of Yule logs and tinselled cribs fills me with horror these days.

Love,

Vera

PS What an awful thing to say about Mabel – I do hope you realised it was only a joke!

22 December

Dear Vera,

I hope this parcel gets to you for Christmas Day at this short notice. It's just a small token – an offcut I picked up in the market, and just hand-rolled the edges, but I know it looks expensive. I was going to give you a couple of my pewter goblets as well, since I've got eight, and I never have more than six round my table now. But I'm not going to send them through the post – it'd cost a fortune.

I'm disappointed at not seeing you at Christmas, but it's my own fault for just assuming and not asking. When Bill mentioned yesterday that it was his mother-in-law he'd be staying with, I immediately understood that it would be quite improper for me to go with him. If I'd only known before, I dare say I could have stayed with you, but only finding out three days before Christmas, I couldn't have imposed.

Anyway, it doesn't matter. I've had to do emergency shopping today, since I hadn't expected to be doing any catering, and quite frankly I am exhausted. I am sitting in Grey's Coffee Lounge at the moment, writing to you prior to wrapping and posting and tracking down some sausage meat. Lesley and Keith, of course, had already arranged to spend Christmas with his parents, but now they're all coming over to me for Boxing Day tea, so it's only me for Christmas dinner, but I would miss the sausage in the stuffing.

Anyway, must get on. There's a queue of people for tables, and I can't spin this coffee out any longer. Have a lovely Christmas. I shouldn't be surprised if you see Bill – he took your telephone number with him and said he might look you up. If you do, wish him a happy Christmas from me. Obviously I can't phone him while he's away. Although I suppose that if he did visit you, he could phone me from your phone. You could tell him to reverse the charges. And it would be nice of course to speak to you too.

Anyway, it's just an idea. Must go now, the waitress is getting edgy. Perhaps hear from you in the near future.

Kindest regards,

Irene

2 January

Dear Irene,

I am so glad you made that unexpected visit on
Christmas Day, even if you did find me up to my elbows
in sage and onion. How lucky your friends happened to be
driving up this way. I do hope the day was pleasanter for
you than it was for me. Frankly I was in that much of a
fluster with Karen just descending out of the blue, and Bill
dropping by at 9.30 on Christmas morning for a sherry, I
didn't know whether I was coming or going! Judging by
the shade of my face when I finally had a moment to
apply some lipstick, I must have been half-cut. Bill's hand
slipped with the sherry bottle! I did find it empty in the
dustbin later. What a shame you missed him.

Boxing Day was much nicer. Bill took us for a run in the
afternoon. We went up to look at the new nuclear power
plant. Actually Karen refused to come. She and Bill had
words over South Africa when we were eating our Stilton
and grapes (I had stupidly left the Outspan sticker on with
the price, but really, she needn't have drawn attention!)
Karen was in a towering rage the whole of the holiday.
When I asked her what was wrong she nearly bit my head
off. She and Kevin are having a 'trial separation', but she
only found out on Christmas Eve.

Bill was very upset he'd missed you. He said you were
a stupid prat not to have phoned him – his mother-in-law
is as deaf as a post. We did have a laugh!

1 feel quite flat now they've all gone home. Kevin rang
on New Year's Day and said the trial was over. Karen said
she supposed he had emptied the deep-freeze by now. She
left this morning with half the turkey. I shall fricassee the
rest and take it round to Mabel. She *would* come out on
New Year's Eve. I was going to a 'do' at the Undertakers'
Hall (they always have such glorious flower arrangements)

but of course I felt I had to stay with Mabel. I saw the New Year in with a glass of Lucozade. Mabel drank her denture water by mistake.

Well – toodle-pip and Happy New Year. Bill said I must pop down and see you both again soon – he even mentioned a holiday cottage weekend.

All the best,

Vera

Two Years Later

28 April

Dear Vera,

I was clearing out my drawers this morning and I came across your letters, and quite frankly I haven't had a moment's peace since. I thought to myself, well, you've got two options, either chuck them out and put it out of your mind, or screw up your courage and write to her. Well, as you can see, I opted for the latter – I couldn't put it out of my mind at all. I've been plunged into soul-searching and depression all day, it just raked it all up again. When I think back now, I feel really stupid and ashamed and if I had my time over again, the whole silly episode wouldn't have been allowed to come to a head. But there you are, it did, and what's done can't be undone. Looking back on it now I think that if only I'd kept my cool and laughed it off (as I notice Marjorie Proops recommended to a girl this week in the *Mirror* who was in a situation similar to mine) then the whole thing would probably have blown over and nothing would have come of it. Anyway, it's no use crying over spilt milk, and we can all be wise after the event.

I don't even know if you're still at the same address, but if you do get this and decide to reply, I'd be overjoyed to hear how you are. I'm still at the same place. I don't think I'll ever move now – I couldn't face the upheaval. Lesley's had a little girl and they're thinking of going to Australia.

All for now in case you're not there. I don't want all my news falling into the wrong hands.

With sincere good wishes,

Irene Spencer

6 May

Dear Irene,

I was so pleased to get your letter. I felt at last that I'd been 'forgiven'. I can't tell you how many anguished sleepless nights I've had over the whole thing – so much so that the doctor had to put me on medication. He said if I went on the way I was doing I would certainly end up in a neck brace. Of course, that fall didn't help – I still have terrible trouble with my lesions. It took me several months to climb out of the 'Slough of Despond', and I was very much aided by literature and music. I've cleaned the library out of Barbara Taylor Bradford, and found Strauss particularly cheering. In fact there was one amusing occasion when the glazier came to replace the picture window and found me waltzing with a moss pole! There weren't many 'highs', however, in the months that followed that incident.

Speaking of which, I want to put your mind at rest once and for all about one thing. Bill and I never meant to end up in bed together. It was all a mistake on the part of the hotel receptionist, who was a deputy stand-in for the Bank Holiday. The hotel did apologise profusely when they saw the trouble they'd caused. They were certainly impressed when Bill hauled the assistant manager over the counter and threatened to unpick his hair weave.

I *did* think the suite was rather palatial when I was shown up, but it was late and I was tired, so I went straight into the adjoining bathroom and started to undress. Unbeknownst to me, Bill was doing the same thing in his adjoining bathroom. There are two in the Honeymoon Suite, you see, I suppose to avoid disappointment. I came out in my nightie, got into bed, put out the light and dozed off without even Barbara Cartland. Bill must have done the same – we never noticed each other, which of course is easily done in a king-size. Imagine how we felt, when suddenly the light snapped on and there you were with your suitcase! Now I know what it must have looked like with Bill wrapped round me like a Russian vine. As he said to me afterwards, he thought I was a bolster – but I don't think that was any reason for you to storm out and refuse to discuss it. I mean, put yourself in my position, in bed with a stranger and without a scrap of make-up. You weren't the only one in shock! Bill gave his knee a terrible wrench leaping out to follow you and goodness knows what the porter made of a man in pyjama bottoms hopping on one foot through the foyer. It wasn't until a week later that it struck me as odd that you'd booked the Honeymoon Suite to begin with. Bill was as mystified as I was. He was under the impression that it was a weekend break for three singles.

I can't deny that it did lead to a greater intimacy between Bill and myself (there's something so endearing about seeing a man in agony), but that went the way of all things, including the picture window.

All I can say is I'm as willing as you are to pick up the pieces. Mabel Thrush is dead, as is the dog, and life can be awfully lonely.

Yours,

Vera

14 May

Dear Vera,

Thank you for your letter, my dear. Although I have no intention of raking up the past, your letter brought it all back – and, of course, told me some things I didn't know – and my first reaction upon reading it was to get in a rage all over again, which I can ill afford with *my* blood pressure, as Dr Prior-Palmer is always pointing out. It's all very well saying don't worry so much and relax, but I've never got to the bottom of how he thinks this is supposed to be done. Anyway.

I did *not* book the Honeymoon Suite. In fact, as Bill well knew at the time, I did not do the booking at all – he did. Or rather his secretary probably did, since as far as I could see he never made a phone call he could avoid, and certainly never *dialled* himself. I remember wondering if he had a septic finger, or if it was a phobia? So *what*, you may ask, was he up to? I have puzzled it over, and can only come up with answers too far-fetched to contemplate. Still. You may say it's all water under the bridge, and I would be the first to agree, particularly as Bill married a girl half his age last year and is now a father again. At his time in life! His son is younger than any of his grandchildren – he's been bragging about it at the golf club, and pretending he's over the moon, but they tell me he looks absolutely haggard. Apparently she's a Women's Libber. Serve him right.

Anyway, I didn't write this letter to talk about him. How are *you*? I'm so sorry to hear about Mabel. You sound a bit down in the mouth. I am free next weekend and the weekend after. Why don't you come on a visit? It would be so pleasant to see you again and discuss old times –

well, some of them. Anyway, let me know your plans and we'll fix the arrangements.

With all best wishes and kindest regards,

Irene

PS I've re-read your letter – what's all this about the picture window going west? Surely not? The best thing about your living room is being able to see out.

16 May

Dear Irene,

I can't come this weekend as it's over to Great Potterton for their Bring and Buy for the disabled, but I could come the weekend after. How about if I came on the Wednesday and stayed till the Tuesday? I'd have to be back then as it's my Scientific and Geographical Society on the 31st, and we're having a talk about Scottish heather. Oh, look at me rushing on and I haven't even said thank you for the kind invitation. Of *course* I'd be glad to keep you company – I'm sure it's very depressing having time on your hands on a Sunday. Did you say Lesley had gone to Australia? Karen and Kevin have split up, did I mention? Karen said finding the crab was the last straw. I don't know to which crab she was referring. Children can be such a worry, especially if they're far away! I haven't seen Howard since he went to live in the country – some village he and his friend found when they walked the Pennine Way. When he told me he was going to Derbyshire I thought he meant for the weekend, not for two years.

Well, must finish as I've got to get 'stuck in' to my gâteaux and fancies for the Bring and Buy. I always do the tea and I pride myself on a glorious spread. Last year I made fifteen puddings. Several are still in the deep-freeze.

See you, all being well, on the 25th.

Warmest regards,

Vera

PS The picture window is a long story and I won't bore you with it now, except to say I was very disappointed. I had always understood reinforced glass was supposed to withstand the heaviest of flung objects.

18 May

Dear Vera,

By all means come on the 25th. I've spent the morning on the phone rejigging my arrangements, and have managed to clear the whole six days, so don't worry, my time is yours. If you want to come by train I can pick you up from the station – I took my driving test last year, and passed with flying colours. I don't know why Clive always told me it was so difficult. Anyway, give me a ring if you want picking up, and I'll be at the station with a red carpet!

Looking forward to catching up,

Best regards,

Irene

20 May

Dear Irene,

I *shall* come on the train, as Karen wrote off my car on
Saturday. She rang me from a lay-by to say she'd had a
little 'prang', as she called it, and could I get the AA out to
help her. Well, needless to say I couldn't get through to
them, and ended up going to fetch her myself in my
neighbour's farm truck. I was half-way down the
motorway before I realised it still had the combine
harvester attached. When I looked at the car I could have
wept. Completely stoved in from bonnet to boot!
Mercifully Karen was alive, though frankly that was a
situation I could cheerfully have altered. I suppose it was
silly of me to get so upset. As Karen said to me as she
dragged me, sobbing, back on to the hard shoulder, 'Oh,
for God's sake, Mother, it's only a car. Claim on the bloody
insurance!' But to me that little Fiesta was like family. I
was closer to it than I've ever been to Karen. I'm intimate
with its internal structure for a start. Anyway, I shall be
arriving on the 3.45 on Wednesday. Never mind the red
carpet, but have a gin and tonic ready!
    Looking forward immensely to seeing you,

All the best till then,

Vera

21 May

Dear Vera,

I'd just nipped down to the village to get some gin after receiving your letter – I don't normally keep it in – when I suddenly remembered the Cricket Club Ladies' Night Dance on Friday. Being the widow of an ex-Vice Captain I am of course expected to attend, and this year I have been chosen to judge the Spot Prize, so I can't let them down. I raced round to see Arthur Snushall, who organises it all and was a great friend of Clive's, and explained the dilemma still clutching the bottle of gin, I realised afterwards, so I don't know what he made of that, and the upshot of it was that he said he'd be delighted to have an extra spare lady, so you're welcome to come. I hope to goodness that you get this in time to organise a long dress as it is formal. I'm in the post office and I'm holding up Mrs Bickerton, so I'd better close.

See you Wednesday!

Irene

1 June

My very dear Irene,

Well, here I am back in *casa mia* and feeling very 'down in the dumps'. Words are inadequate (they so frequently *are* aren't they?) to express my thanks for such a splendidly enjoyable time. I've often thought penning an opera the only really satisfactory way of expressing great emotion. Sadly I am not gifted in that direction, though Karen once rudely remarked that I lived my life as though it were one. Which reminds me, you're a dark horse, keeping quiet about that nice young curate, Bruce, until he appeared at Sunday lunchtime! That was a merry gathering, wasn't it? I do hope he was all right for Evensong. I don't care what people say about 'High' or 'Low', the clergy should always be accessible. He reminded me of Gideon, a young man I was once in love with. He took me to the tennis club New Year's Eve dance and we made many revelations to each other in the back of his Baby Austin. The next day he dropped in a note informing me he was taking holy orders. Of course, I was very young myself at the time – this was 1937.

What a charmer Arthur Snushall is! He apologised so profusely, I don't know how you have the heart to still be angry with him. It was an honest mistake and easily made when you are three sheets to the wind, or perhaps, in Arthur's case, three and a half. I thoroughly enjoyed presenting the prize, even though the winning couple had stepped on my fishtail (thank heavens I still have the use of Mabel Thrush's Singer) and I was quite at a loss with the jokes about legside wides and maiden overs. Gerald wasn't a cricket player.

In fact all your friends were very hospitable and pleasant. I don't know why you warned me about Dorothy Bickerstaff. She had nothing but kind words to say about you, including that Clive had led you a dog's life and you'd made an amazing recovery. Your cooking was . . . well, what can I say? *Prolific*. Don't forget to put in that recipe for the mulled wine – your curate certainly enjoyed it! Oh dear, the phone is ringing . . .

That was Karen. Apparently she is coming on a visit. She *never* comes this time of year – it's always August for my birthday, or Christmas. She was as brief as ever. As soon as I said I'd be there to meet the train, she slammed down the receiver. I *do* hope . . . oh well, never mind. Better close now as I must scurry round and get some food in, also remember to put up the picture she gave me last Christmas and remove Kevin from the wedding photo.

With a million thanks,

Toodle-pip,

Vera

PS I've just thought what the opera would be called – of course, *The Merry Widow*!

4 June

Dear Vera,

You may not be aware that my maiden name was Onions. When I was a child I tried to honour my father and my mother, who sacrificed everything for my education at Tavistock Road School for Girls, by working hard and trying to excel, despite the fact that I have never been a top-notch intellectual. I am sure that you can imagine my gratified delight, therefore, when in my last year, after striving for recognition for so long, I was awarded an inscribed and beautifully bound copy of the King James Bible for Neatness. I can remember to this day the pride with which I took my place on the platform to receive it from Miss Frobisher herself in my darned but immaculate school uniform and, for the occasion, a borrowed pair of white kid gloves. The school hall resounded with cheers, and I was happier then than I have ever been. On returning to my place, however, pressed by the girls to show them my award, I opened the book at the inscribed plate only to see not my name but Irene Springthorpe's, the girl who had head lice in 4B. On being informed of the reason for my distress, Miss Frobisher assured me it was an obvious error, and offered to have it scratched out and amended, but as it was a prize for neatness I naturally declined. They say that pride comes before a fall, but in my case it was simultaneous. Even though I look at that Bible every day, I can never open it without being filled with a sense of cruel injustice.

The handing out of the Spot Prizes this year at the Ladies' Night Dinner Dance was to have been an honour bestowed upon me by the Club in recognition of my doing the catering for the players' refreshment for twenty-five years, and carrying on to this day despite my husband not playing for the team after he died three years ago. I can forgive Arthur his mistake, since, as he said himself, he was wearing the wrong glasses, but I find it very difficult to come to terms with your selfishness in not pointing it out, and just capitalising on it to hog the limelight.

Another thing you might be amused by is that your friend Dorothy Bickerstaff has every reason to say that Clive led me a dog's life, considering she was the bitch who led him astray when Lesley was teething and I had temporarily let myself go. Trust you to like her. You are so easily taken in.

As for your allegations about Bruce and myself, I can assure you that our relations go no further than his kind offer to help me out over a couple of sticky points in St Paul's Epistle to the Ephesians. When he came round this morning and found me crying tears of rage over your letter, he pointed out to me St Paul's wisdom (Ch. 4, v. 26) 'Let not the sun go down upon your wrath', so you've got him to thank that I have taken the trouble to write you this response, to give you the opportunity of apologising. Left to my own devices I would more probably have followed the teaching in verse 27, 'Neither give place to the devil', and just severed our connection. Incidentally, Bruce is an unswerving teetotal, so if your memory of Sunday's lunch is that he was enjoying my mulled wine in a ribald manner, I think it wiser not to enclose the recipe. Perhaps you are trying to model yourself too closely on the 'Merry Widow'? I trust you will take this letter in the spirit it is intended, and that you will try to have more thought for others instead of sailing gaily through their lives, treading on their corns.

Kind regards,

Irene

12 June

Dear Irene,

I hardly know how to respond to your last. I had no idea I was giving such offence. My 'jokey' tone was an attempt (misplaced, I now see) to jolly you out of the doldrums you were in during the latter half of my visit. I'm sure a little harmless teasing cannot alone have produced this response and can only think there is something else going on of a 'personal' nature . . . perhaps involving that nice young curate? By the by, I certainly didn't mean to imply that he was a toper, not that that in itself would be unusual in the cloth. The vicar who married Gerald and myself could hardly stand up – if it comes to that, neither could Gerald – and was seen at the reception with a bottle of sherry under one arm and a bridesmaid under the other. But I digress . . .

On re-reading your letter, I'm reminded of the dreadful time that I fell out with my (ex) best friend Muriel. She was convinced I was 'after' her boyfriend, which was utter nonsense. It was all a mistake, which came about when I wore one of her frocks to a party. She didn't speak to me for a month and I was so upset I actually contemplated suicide and went as far as an overdose of my mother's indigestion tablets. Thirteen is such an emotive age, isn't it?

I *am* sorry about your awful childhood. It excuses a lot. I told myself again how lucky I was – my father may have been tyrannical but he was a natural musician. And of course I was always at the centre of a group of friends and admirers. Speaking of which, Eric Glendower is coming up the path so I must finish this later . . .

He wanted me to sponsor him for a swim. I said yes, as I'm sure he'll never go over three lengths – his pacemaker couldn't take it. Last week Mavis Peake cost me an arm

and a leg on a sponsored ice dance for pensioners.
Actually she cost herself an arm and a leg also – during
the rumba she fell over and broke her wrist and her ankle.
It's been a week for breakages – Karen dropped my best
Denbighware casserole on the floor on Sunday and
scattered it and its contents (chicken à la king) to the four
winds . . . or perhaps I should say, the four walls – I
scraped most of it off the paintwork. She said I made her
jump, but I ask you, if you can't go into your own kitchen
without knocking, where can you go?! I didn't say
anything. The fact is she was jumpy as a cat all weekend.
She's obviously got something on her mind, but I'll be the
last to know it.

Well, my dear, I do hope this has put the record straight
between us. I'm sure in a saner moment you will realise
how highly I value our friendship. As I said to Karen at
the weekend, I had no idea women could be so close. At
last I know what it is to have a sister. She gave me her
usual scornful glance and said where had I been for the
last twenty years – had I *heard* of the women's movement?

Hoping you feel better soon,

Very best wishes,

Vera

20 June

Dear Vera,

Where are you? I've been trying to phone and you're *never* in. I have been living under a cloud for weeks, and now the worst has happened. Keith got the job he was after in Wollongong, New South Wales. Right up until the last minute I thought he wouldn't get it – I know for a fact that his spelling is shocking, but apparently that is what secretaries are for and it doesn't seem to matter in top jobs if you are illiterate or not. It was touch and go up to the last minute as there was a chap from Huddersfield they really wanted more than Keith, but then he found out he was HIVES positive so he didn't want to leave his family. What sort of a company is it who would be taken in by a man like that in the first place? Anyway, by the time they'd sorted all that lot out everything had to happen at once, and Lesley and Keith left yesterday and took my baby girl. What sort of a country is that to bring a child up in?

When I think of all we sacrificed for Lesley – years ago Clive could have taken a very well-paid job in Croydon, London, but we didn't take it because we didn't want her growing up a street urchin in a big city. How will they ever find a baby-sitter that they can trust? The stories you read in the papers today, you can't trust anybody outside the family to look after your children, and even inside the family it seems there is a minefield of danger if there are male members. I won't see her grow up, and by the time I get to see her again she'll be talking with that dreadful accent.

And there was never any question of them asking me what I thought, or of asking me to go with them. I shouldn't have gone anyway, as I think young people have to be left alone to make their own mistakes. I could cheerfully throttle Lesley, and I know if Clive had been alive he'd have knocked their heads together. And what about her schooling? Her qualifications won't be worth the paper they're written on. And what about when she gets ill? Would you like to be operated on by a foreign doctor? I know I wouldn't. And what about eating? The food will all be different, and Cheryl Marie is so faddy, and with Lesley for a mother she'll have faded to nothing before she notices.

I'm absolutely beside myself and I've been sobbing for days. I think there ought to be a law against people taking the children out of the family. Wilfully wicked and adulterous parents are allowed rights, but you never hear about the rights of the grandparents, which is ridiculous when you think that all of the Law Lords must be grandparents themselves. Not to see my baby grow up is the cruellest thing Lesley could ever do to me, and she's done some things in her time. When she went to college it had to be the other end of the country.

And I'm just supposed to clean up the mess. They've left me with her house to sell, and I've to arrange shipment of various bits of furniture. Why couldn't Lesley have stayed to do that herself? And how irresponsible for the three of them to fly out on the same plane – you'd never catch the royal family doing that, and, let's face it, they are seasoned air travellers.

I've just tried ringing you again but you're still not answering. It's five a.m. and it's too late to go to bed now. I couldn't sleep anyway, despite the brandy I've taken to dull my emotion. I have never felt so alone. I am even questioning whether there is a God, which I am sure Bruce could put my mind at rest on if he wasn't on a retreat in the Holy Land. Please come and help me out, Vera, I really need a friend and you know I don't ask for favours lightly.

My brandy glass has just shattered in my hand for no apparent reason, hence the blood on the first page.

Everything is going against me. I'd ring the Samaritans but I don't know their number. Lesley just rang, bubbling over, to say they'd arrived safely. She seems incapable of grasping the fact that if I'd been asleep she'd have woken me up. I suppose now I'm going to have to face years of sleepless nights wondering if she's going to ring. She wouldn't put Cheryl Marie to the phone, but I could hear crying in the background. I knew she wouldn't be happy there. What can I do?

Yours in distress,

Irene

24 June

My dear Irene,

I nearly wept when I read your letter. To be honest, I had plenty to weep about. You couldn't get me as I was away, looking after Karen. I was rung up in the middle of the night last Tuesday by some hospital orderly saying they'd found my name in Karen's Filofax under 'Next of kin' (after Auntie Madge, who's dead, and Uncle Dick, who's an alcoholic) and could I come immediately? Of course I jumped straight to the conclusion that she'd been in a frightful accident, aided by the orderly, who told me she was dying. Turned out he'd said *crying*, but the combination of middle-of-the-night confusion and foreign accent had me running to the car and driving all the way to the hospital, exceeding the speed limit and wearing my reading glasses. I have only once before covered ground so fast and that was on a pair of out-of-control skis in the Cairngorms.

The hospital was in semi-darkness (I believe they are economising on electricity – couldn't get a cup of tea for love nor money) and a very junior night-nurse eventually located Karen for me, not, thank God, in the mortuary, but in the Margaret Hilda Roberts ward, a desolate room empty but for a single bed and a do-it-yourself First Aid kit. Karen was asleep and was not very pleased when I shook her awake. She said what on earth was I doing there, and when I told her I'd been summoned she snorted something about 'bloody stupid red tape' and turned over. It was hours before I could get any further information, or indeed a cup of tea.

I don't know if I dare tell you the rest. Oh, Irene, what a blessing it is that you're such a good friend . . . and so far away. If I confided this to anyone here, it would be round the village in seconds. Karen finally told me the truth. She is pregnant.

I had to stop and have a stiff whisky. I don't know what's the matter with me, I must be in shock. I'd describe my symptoms as menopausal, if all that weren't far behind me. In fact Karen didn't tell me, the ward sister did when she came on duty next morning. She explained that Karen had been rushed to hospital with a suspected miscarriage. They'd needed to give her a blood transfusion and as they didn't have any handy, they'd phoned next of kin (me) to see if I could donate some. I was rolling up my sleeve when she said not to worry, they'd found some frozen in the canteen fridge and they were confident that would do her.

I can't describe to you my horror, rage, despair, etc. I had no idea. As you know, Karen has been estranged from her husband for over two years now. They *have* met on occasion, but only with a solicitor present.

I sat with her until she came to again, but I couldn't bring myself to touch her. When she woke up her first question was whether she'd lost the baby. I said unfortunately not, but we'd just have to grin and bear it. She told me not to be so F-word stupid, she wanted the baby desperately and was delighted she hadn't miscarried. I'm afraid I lost my temper and shouted at her. I don't know what I said. Years of pent-up grief came out, starting with the time, aged three, she'd smashed a doll I'd had since *I* was a baby. She just stared at me and when I dried up said I'd better make use of my hospital trip to visit the psychiatrist. I retorted that I hoped the blood transfusion hadn't been infected, but in any case the baby would probably have hooves as it had come from a pound of calves' liver. The awful things one says in the heat of the moment! Of course she broke down and cried and then the sister came along and said they needed the bed and could I take her home now? That's where I've been ever since.

I'm so wrapped up in my own anguished misery, I've got nothing left over for other people. I can't face going out of doors and certainly couldn't stand the strain of travelling on public transport. You are welcome to come to me, my dear, and I'll do my best to cheer you, but I feel I must warn you to be prepared for a sorry wrung-out dishcloth.

Yours, as ever,

Vera

4 July

Dear Vera,

The journey back was the worst in living memory. I had to stand all the way to Crowick while 'businessmen' had seats paid for by their companies for the tax relief. I have torn up my Pensioners' Railcard and have sent half to the Ministry of Transport and half to Mrs Thatcher, with covering letters demanding a refund and reminding them that it was people like me who voted them in. Never again! I feel quite 'militant' after my talks with Karen, and will certainly be writing more letters of a complaining nature in future. The only nice part of the return itinerary was a most charming West Indian bus conductor who has just joined our 41 bus route at home, and who helped me with my case. I'm very much looking forward to travelling with him again.

I hope your spirits have remained up since I left, and I'm quite sure once you see your grandchild you'll see how wrong you were to be upset over its coming. Nothing can compare to a grandmother's joy over the birth of the first: a baby of your very own without the usual messy and inconvenient ways of getting it. No news from Wollongong on my return incidentally, but what did I expect? Lesley has no idea I visited you. As far as she's concerned I could have been lying here dead since the 20th ult.

I enclose a card for Karen for you to forward if necessary, as I don't know where she'll be staying. I've sealed it, but there is no big mystery – just a 'get well' and 'congratulations' combined.

Remember what I said about Christmas, and start looking at the catalogues. If we go early and come back early, we'll be back in plenty of time before Karen needs you. And forget Saga – I don't want to be stuck with a load of old people.

With kindest regards, your friend,

Irene

PS I had forgotten to cancel the milk. Am sending some cream cheese under separate cover. Hope first-class post is working!

4 July

My dear Karen,

Just a little 'thank-you' note for all our lovely chats. If I had a daughter like you I'd count myself as truly blessed – I can't think what your mother finds to complain about. Try to be kind to her, dear; our generation had different ideas about things, and not all of us have managed to adapt our way of thinking as yet. I've thought over your little problem quite a bit, and I stick by what I said before – don't tell her till after it's born. You never know, it might be very pale, and she might never need to be any the wiser. I know for a fact she has racist tendencies, since she wrote to me recently about a 'foreign accent' in an unflattering way, so it's as well to keep your own counsel till she's had time to fall in love with it. In the meantime, I'll try to drop the odd casual mention about the plus side of our Commonwealth friends. Don't hesitate to ring me if you need a chat.

Fondest wishes,

Rene

10 July

Dear Irene,

Yesterday a large pot of cream cheese was delivered by
parcel post. When I say 'delivered', I mean flung out of a
post office vehicle cruising at approx. 75 m.p.h. down the
wrong side of the road. Fortunately I wasn't standing on
the doorstep, so escaped most of the resulting explosion.
The hydrangea took the full force of the blast and I was
half an hour with the hosepipe ridding it of a substance
reminiscent of the droppings of an incontinent pterodactyl
(did I mention we were on to dinosaurs in my Natural
History lectures?). It wasn't until I got your letter this
morning – six days by first-class post – that I realised what
a kind thought had gone astray. I'm sure it would have
been delicious. As it was, I had to give my hair three
washes and my gardening gloves are fit for the dustbin.

Karen is much better thank you. I passed on your card. I
think you do right to seal everything, given the current state
of the post office, though I did think sticky tape *and* sealing
wax was going a bit far. I'm sure she was pleased, though
she hasn't mentioned. Too busy wondering whether sheep's
yoghurt has Listerine in it. She says she won't touch
anything that could harm the 'unborn foetus'. I ask you,
what a way to talk about your first baby! I said to her, if you
worried about everything you ate, you'd end up starving.
She said she supposed I wanted her to go polluting the
'unborn foetus' with meat force-fed on excrement. I don't
know where she gets her lavatorial expressions. Though,
come to think of it, Gerald did keep a secret diary . . .

She's got a library of books on child care – I pointed out
she is only eight weeks pregnant – and says she is
bringing the baby up 'green'. I said that would certainly be
preferable to black, but she gave me such a funny look I
had to explain I was joking.

I keep turning over and over in my mind where I've gone wrong with Karen. My own father threatened to horsewhip me if I ever brought home 'trouble'. He was a powerful man but had a wonderful sense of humour. The vicar's sermon this week was all about how dead friends and relations can see us and what we're doing. My father must be turning in his grave – thank God he was short-sighted. I mentioned it to Karen, but she told me not to be 'mawkish'. Thank heavens for Howard! At least I have one child I can be proud of. I enclose a note from Karen which has just arrived. I must remember to pass on your address, and will close now as I think I have a migraine coming on. I have been too depressed to go to the travel agent.

Yours,

Vera

PS *You've* obviously cheered up if you can banter words with the bus conductor. I've tried chatting to mine – mostly about the state of the bus service – but he's a surly brute.

PPS What 'militant' talks did you have with Karen?

8 July

Dear Rene,

Thanks for the advice – much appreciated. Haven't said a word to Mum – you know what she's like. Will ring soon. Can't visit anyone at the mo' due to morning sickness.

Cheers,

Karen

24 July

My dear Vera,

Just a brief note to see if you've received the Caribbean holiday brochures I sent you. I've tried phoning but only get that continuous tone that usually denotes an unpaid bill! I am very busy organising a Bring and Buy and a non-stop 48-hour KeepFitathon at the church hall against the proposed siting of a nuclear dump under the golf links at Grossthorpe. Feelings are running very high here in Hethergreen and surrounding districts, and everybody is pulling their weight, including the cricket team, who are all keen golfers to a man, and who are doing a sponsored pub crawl. Arthur's just been round for his sponsorship and was very insistent that I gave him your address. Hope you don't mind. Must fly as Bruce and I are having a breakfast meeting this morning to discuss strategy over the tombola. Postcard from Lesley yesterday saying that they love it over there. Typical.

Fondest regards,

Irene

28 July

Dear Irene,

You are right to keep yourself busy, it's the best cure for desperation. I have scoured the house from top to bottom and finally tackled Gerald's cupboard, which I haven't been able to touch since he died. It took me an hour to prise off the padlock and then I wished I had let well alone. I found some things of a deeply distressing nature, of which I will only say that I now see where Karen gets her depraved behaviour. Howard, thank God, has always favoured my side. He is such a dear. His invitation to visit the Derby Dales came just in the nick of time and I am off there for the weekend. I shall take the brochures to pore over at leisure. I've opened a couple, but somehow all those pineapples just make me feel bilious.

Have a couple for me on your pub crawl,

All the best,

Vera

PS My phone has been off the hook as I have been getting 'nuisance' calls.

30 July

My poor dear Vera,

I am writing post-haste to simply say 'confide in me'. I had a similar experience over Clive's last effects. Write to me and tell me everything. Any chance of letting me have the less offensive artefacts for my Bring and Buy?

All my warmest wishes and sympathy,

Irene

Irene Spencer

34 Wormwold Way

Hethergreen

Dear Irene,

Howard has assured me that what I found was no more than Gerald's Masonic Regalia.

The Derby Dales are wonderfully refreshing, as you can see from this picture. Majestic vistas and quite delightful dwellings. Howard and Antony live in a converted sheep bothy. They are turning it into an Alternative Health and Therapy centre and I must say I never knew there were so many different textile! Am writing this from the pub next door where I'm downing a pint of 'Shepherd's ruin'.

Feeling much more cheerful,
Yours as ever
Vera

'Rainstorm Over Shap', photo by Scott Godber.

19 August

Dear Vera,

What a hectic and happy few days I've had having Karen here! Shopping became a joy again. She's such a lovely girl, I really can't imagine why the two of you don't click better. I hope you've got over having the hump with us now – I had no idea she was planning to visit, and I don't think *she* did till she was half-way up the motorway. It just so happened that she was giving me a foot massage when you rang, so naturally it was all a bit giggly. I don't know where you get your conspiracy ideas from – Karen said you've been watching too much *Dynasty*!

I'm really writing to find out your views on the Caribbean hols. If we don't book soon we'll be bitterly disappointed and end up going somewhere we don't like with no bathroom facilities. Karen says that St Kitts is particularly nice, or so a friend told her. It certainly looks ravishingly pleasant in the brochure (page 31 – I particularly like the look of Harry's Hideaway – what about those bananas!)

I was pleased to hear in your last that Gerald's worst fault was being a Mason. One day if I get really tiddly, I'll tell you what I found out about Clive whilst sifting through his effects. You think you know somebody after forty years of marriage, only to find you'd been in utter ignorance. When I think back over how blind and naive I was – but I'm just playing into the hands of my hypertension. Karen told me that when I feel myself getting het up, I should change the subject and dwell on something pleasant.

1 hope you don't mind, but she confided in me about Howard. I must admit I had started to wonder. I think you're marvellous, accepting it so naturally. I talked it over with Bruce from a religious point of view, but he was very

noncommittal. According to him you can argue it both ways, depending on which biblical texts you choose as your reference. But I suppose when you're looking to have your own parish in the near future, you have to be very circumspect about controversy.

It seems strange to me that you can forgive Howard for the way he is, but can't seem to come to grips with Karen. I mean, any girl can make one mistake and 'catch her toe', but Howard must be sinning on a nightly basis. Is it because he's your son, do you think? I've always been very grateful for not having had a boy – I know I would have spoiled him to death. I suppose that most boys in Howard's predicament have had a very emotional relationship with their mothers.

Arthur Snushall has just nipped in to collect his sponsor money. It cost me half a week's pension – they managed to crawl round eighty-three pubs! He wanted to tell me all about it, but I cut him off. He can be a bore sometimes, even though he'd do anything for you. You obviously made a big impact on him at the Ladies' Night. He was most insistent that I send you his warmest regards, and wonders when you'll be coming to stay again. Of course you know, I'm sure, that he's very happily married.

The house feels very empty without Karen, and I'm starting to have wanderlust again. If you're still feeling bilious I could come and look after you for a few days if you like. I could manage next week or the week after, but not the week after that, as that is when they are sending the bulldozers in and we're having a sit-in on the eighteenth tee. I don't know *what* I'll wear.

Hurry up and decide about our hols!

Warmest regards,

Irene

25 August

Dear Irene,

I got stuck in the automatic bus doors on Friday and was cursed by the driver in fluent Caribbean. I've quite gone off it for a holiday – I'm not at all sure it's the right kind of 'colourful'. Perhaps you should take Karen, as you seem to get on so well with her. She would jump at the chance of a free ride – she's always known a soft touch when she saw one. You could continue your confidences in Harry's Hideaway, where I'm sure the bananas would come in useful. Frankly, one look at them would turn a Sumo wrestler bilious.

As for your obscure remarks about Howard, they are both puzzling and hurtful. I've always known Karen was deeply jealous of her brother (it started when they were children – he was sensitive and clever, as well as better-looking) but I had no idea she went round fabricating stories about his 'relationship' with me. What on earth is she suggesting? Personally, I can't see a thing wrong with 'the way he is'. Vegetarianism is becoming all the vogue. This week I've done several wonderful things with a cauli, and if you consider a few pints of 'local brew' after a hard day's Colonic Irrigation 'sinning', then you are even more narrow-minded than I thought. Perhaps Bruce isn't the only one who's thinking to have his own parish?

I'm afraid it's not convenient for you to visit at the moment, as I've invited Audrey Roscoe. She's such good company, always up for a gossip and a giggle. I must tell you what she said about Clive sometime. Good luck with the sit-in. I should wear that bathing costume you 'impulse'-bought last summer. Should be enough to frighten a bulldozer.

Yours,

Vera

PS I've discovered it is Arthur Snushall who's been making the 'nuisance' calls. If his wife thinks she's happily married, I can only say 'poor creature'.

The Manse
The Green
Hethergreen

6 October

Dear Mrs Small,

I wonder if you remember meeting me at the luncheon table of our mutual friend, Mrs Irene Spencer? I found your address in her book and take the liberty of writing, which intrusion I hope you will forgive in the circumstances.

You may be aware that we in Hethergreen and surrounding parishes mounted a demonstration against the building of a nuclear waste dumping site under the golf links at Grossthorpe a few weeks ago, but you may not have read in the newspapers of the consequences of this peaceful protest on our part. I enclose a cutting from the *Micklechester Mercury*. The lady in question was our mutual friend.

Irene came out of her coma early last week and most of the injuries (fortunately bruises and grazes) are nearly completely healed. However, she is suffering from almost total amnesia, and since she is to be returned to the community soon, I am wondering if you might help. I know that she regards you as her closest friend – in fact, her first (and only) words on regaining consciousness were, 'You told me it'd frighten the bulldozer, Vera!' – perhaps you know what she meant. Since then she has become a deaf mute.

The doctors at the Micklechester Royal Infirmary feel that if her old friends were to remind her, as it were, of themselves and their common experiences, then her memory and her ability to communicate might be restored. Personally I am hardly surprised that her experiences have rendered her speechless. I have telephoned her daughter in Australia, but unfortunately she is unable to come over at the moment, due to an important Beach Barbecue she had been planning for her husband's birthday.

Could you find time to jot her a few lines about yourself – and indeed herself? If you cast your mind about, I am sure you can find many suitable memories – even if it were only to talk about the war, which inevitably made a great impression on people of your generation. My own acquaintance with her is unfortunately too short to have made much impression on her consciousness, and when she does seem to recognise me at all, she appears to mouth 'Clive'. Would you know who that might be?

It seems she kept herself rather to herself in the parish, and whereas she is not exactly without friends, there is nobody locally who knows her intimately. I do hope you may be able to help, as I am soon to take up my duties in my new parish of Cynnington some hundred miles away, and it would be a comfort to know that a good friend was taking responsibility for her recovery.

God bless and keep you,

Yours,

Bruce

REV. BRUCE SPRINGTHORPE

SEX-MAD GRANNY NUKES BULLDOZER

DRUG-crazed hippies went on the rampage at Grossthorpe Golf Club yesterday, damaging a bulldozer and turning the green grass of the eighteenth tee into blood-soaked furrows.

Greenkeeper Jack Maythorpe wept as he described the carnage. 'It'll be six months before anybody can play a ball on that surface,' he said, as he was led away by grieving relations.

The unprovoked mayhem started at 10.00 a.m. when CEGB workmen went peacefully about their business of building a much needed dumping site for spent fuel rods underneath the Grossthorpe links.

CEGB had planned to remove and replace the turf and topsoil after burying the waste, thereby preserving the ecological balance – a dream now shattered by the ruthless damage done to the green by the hundreds of NIMBY (Not In My Back Yard) hippies' unsuitable footwear ripping it to shreds.

Further damage was done when a sex-mad granny (83), as yet unnamed, wearing only a multi-coloured lurex bathing costume and high heels, maliciously headbutted a bulldozer driven by Mr Ken Haggard.

'She came at me like a screaming fury,' said Mr Haggard, who is now being treated for shock at Micklechester Royal, 'waving her arms in a threatening manner. I had been ordered to pursue my duties and it was more than my job was worth to down tools.' Allegations by the hippies that the ageing beauty queen had been trying to warn Mr Haggard of a small child in his path have proved groundless.

Inspector Gravers of Micklechester CID, in charge of the investigation, is waiting for her to help the police with their enquiries. 'At the moment she is suffering from psychosomatic unconsciousness which is all in her head,' said the Inspector, a keen student of psychology in his spare time, 'which in my experience is a sure sign of a psychopathic mind unable to come to terms with their own guilt after an act of violence.'

Turn to page 35 for results and reports on the Netherthorpe Amateur Golfing Championships.

9 October

Dear Rev. Springsteen,

I was horrified by your letter. It was I who advised Irene to meet trouble head on – needless to say, I never expected her to take me quite so literally. I will write to her straight away, though our 'shared past' is limited to a couple of years. I've no idea what she was doing in the war, though she did mutter darkly once about her war being 'wasted'.

Of course I remember meeting you. We talked about the gay priesthood and Cliff Richard and you told me you were setting the 23rd Psalm to rock music. Good luck in your new billet – I hope they appreciate flair. I still remember the shocking-pink shirt under the dog collar! Irene will miss you dreadfully, of course. That is, she would if she knew who you were. Clive is her deceased husband and I've always had the impression she doesn't miss him at all. Perhaps, in her troubled mind, she is returning to the early days of their courtship when she sees you. You know, I am sure, that she had a soft spot for you. It must be a bitter blow for you too, to leave her, especially in such a state, but 'The Lord giveth and the Lord taketh away', as she once said to me when I mislaid my dentures.

God bless you too,

Yours faithfully,

Vera Small

9 October

My Dearest Irene (you do remember your name, I hope!)

I'm so sorry to hear of your plight. It's one thing having the odd lapse (I frequently forgot who Gerald was when I had to introduce him) but quite another living in a total void. I've enclosed a few things that might jog your brain waves. The photograph of us was taken at Lesley's (your daughter's) wedding – I'm the one with the sherry trifle in my hand. The other artefacts might put you in mind of Clive, though Gerald was a larger man altogether.

Now . . . where to start? Perhaps at the beginning (as you are, as it were, a clean sheet to be written on!). I was seventeen when war broke out. I was in the hen-house at the bottom of our yard, looking for Clara, who'd gone very broody, and I'd just bent over to see if she was hiding behind the hutch when I felt a sharp pinch on my bottom and a loud voice said, 'Better keep that well covered now the Hun is coming.' Well, of course it was our next-door neighbour, Ray Hatchett, who was a devil for catching you unawares. I had to be very careful when I was hanging out the washing. I must have gone the colour of my jumper (Schiaparelli shocking, as it came to be known later) because he said, 'Now, now, girl, this is no time to have a stroke. We've just declared war on Hitler.' I dropped everything and ran straight into the house to make sure my mother was all right. She was sitting with her ear glued to the radio and gravy was dripping down the wall from where my father had just flung his dinner. Silly isn't it, the things you remember?

I saw my boyfriend, Charlie, that evening. He was wondering if his hammer toe would delay his call-up papers. We danced until dawn at the tennis club (that is, I did – Charlie couldn't because of his hammer toe) and all the girls were crying. That Monday I gave in my notice at the milliner's where I'd been training and declared myself free for war work. Well, my dear, that's enough for now. I don't want to tire you. Write as soon as you remember how to hold a pen and meanwhile here's a couple of 'teasers' for you . . .

Caribbean holidays.

Karen's baby.

All the very best for a swift recovery,

Love,

Vera Small

20 October

Dear Mrs Small,

Thank you for your kind letter, which the hospital forwarded to me today. It must have arrived on the day I left, and then got snarled up in the system somewhere. There was quite a lot of blood on the envelope, which makes me wonder if it went to Casualty.

I stumbled on some other letters of yours the other day and I was wondering if you'd crop up again, since we have obviously shared some turbulent times. It looks from the last letter you wrote me before the accident as if I upset you in some way, for which I can only apologise and assure you that, as far as I'm concerned, the 'hatchet' is well and truly buried. Clive was my husband – I know that from the irrefutable evidence I've found around the house, particularly a wedding photo – but then, I've also found another wedding photo where I appear to be getting married, so perhaps I was a bigamist. You say in that letter that a lady called Audrey Roscoe told you some amusing stories about Clive – could you share them with me, in case it strikes a chord?

I have got to grips with the fact that I have a daughter called Lesley, as she has phoned me a couple of times in the middle of the night. I can't say I'm much drawn to her, which is a dreadful thing for a mother to say, but she has a very shrill edge to her voice and seems to think I am to blame for everything that's ever happened to her. Bruce, a very nice vicar who seems to be a bit light on his feet and has been taking care of me, has obviously asked her, like you, to refresh my memory over certain incidents, and honestly, if I've been as wicked to her as she tries to make out, it's a wonder the NSPCC didn't send me to the gallows years ago. Apparently, she moved to Australia so she wouldn't have to see me, but on the strength of her nocturnal accusations, all I can say is 'good riddance'.

I see from the newspapers that I used to be 'sex-mad', but I can't say I've had many stirrings since. My solicitor says that if it's not back in a couple of weeks, we must sue for loss of sex drive, but I don't know if it's worth the fuss. Apparently I'm in enough trouble already without aggravating the police. I'm to be charged with obstructing the CEGB in the pursuit of their duties, and wilful damage to a bulldozer, which all sounds a bit far-fetched to me. But then, every time I pick up a paper or turn on the television, things seem to be far-fetched. Are we supposed to believe the things they say in Parliament when they say it, or wait until the next day when they say they didn't say it, in fact they'd said the opposite?

It was interesting to read your reminiscences about the war, and it reminded me that the day war broke out I started my periods, which seemed to me to be much more important at the time. My best friend Dolly had started hers when she was twelve, and I at thirteen thought womanhood would never come to me. As you say, the things you remember!

Thank you for the brain-teasers. Caribbean holidays is easy, as it was in your last letter that you didn't want to go any more due to a misunderstanding with a black bus driver. Obviously we'd been planning to go. Karen's baby is harder, but I think I've got to the bottom of it. It was a film where everybody was pleased when she got pregnant, but when it was born they realised it was the devil. Am I close?

I hope you write to me again soon. Everybody round here seems a bit embarrassed that I don't know them, but you seem much more fun. I hope the second time around, you choose me for your friend again. Can I call you Vera in my next?

With love and gratitude,

Irene Spencer

30 October

My dear Irene,

I was very touched by your last. Of course you can call me Vera. In fact, I used to be known to my intimates as 'Vee' – all the girls at the dockyard had nicknames. Talking to you about the war has set off a lot of reminiscences. I even got an old photograph album out of the attic and had a flick through. I did laugh. Those trousers! We all seemed so happy, you wouldn't have thought there was a war on. I couldn't put a name to all of the faces, but I did remember Gerald (my husband) who was jolly good-looking in uniform, but terribly wet at kissing. Which brings me to your point about sex-drive. I never knew I had one until Gerald died, but looking at those pictures brought it all back to me. I felt a most peculiar stirring (I hope you don't mind my getting personal . . . it might be useful for your solicitor); it was something like a hot flush, but pleasanter. In fact, I had to have a cold shower. It was the window cleaner's day and I didn't want him to arrive and find me all of a dither.

I got quite angry thinking about all we'd missed. When I look at Karen . . .! (Karen's baby, by the way, will be my first grandchild and, as far as I know, she hasn't been dabbling in black magic.) In our day girls had to behave 'properly'. My father would have hit the roof, or rather his dinner would, if he'd found out I was 'going' with anyone. Between you and me, that didn't entirely stop me. I read *Forever Amber* when I was fourteen and there were one or two very steamy scenes on our annual chapel picnics. I particularly remember rolling in bluebells with Cecil, who became a dentist. Of course, the girls at the dockyard were devils at egging each other on. We gave our boss a very hard time, always grabbing handfuls of him. You see, they weren't types I'd have met in civvy

street . . . some of them were quite common. I got a
graphic introduction to sex from Greta, one day when I
was sent on an errand to the boiler room. There she was
in a cloud of steam, with Bob Biggin going at it like a road
drill. Of course, he was a power tool operator.

You see, I was rather sheltered from 'life', apart from the
cats and the chickens. My mother was a very reserved
woman and never mentioned anything 'personal'. The day
my periods started, I was too frightened to tell her. I
stuffed a wad of newspaper from the lav down my
knickers and ran down the road to my schoolfriend
Jeannie, who gave me an aspirin and the 'doings'. Till the
day she died my mother never knew I menstruated.
Heaven knows where she thought I got Karen and
Howard! I sometimes wonder that myself. Not Howard, of
course, he's a darling, but I do so wish he'd settle down
and have children. Trust it to be Karen who's producing!

What a shame Lesley has taken that attitude. I don't
know. You worry yourself sick over daughters and they
only throw it back in your face. I remember sitting up all
night to make Karen a lovely little frock for a party. She
went to it wearing black tights, a black skirt and Gerald's
long black sweater. She looked like the bride of Dracula.
Of course, if I said anything, her lip would curl and she
would spit, 'I can't go round like Little Bo Peep – times
have changed, Mother'. Yes indeed, times have changed –
but people haven't, as I would frequently tell her.
Divorced, pregnant and abandoned by her lover, she's
found out that one the hard way.

Well, my dear, all for now. I hope you're eating plenty
of fish. Let me know if you'd like a visit.

Yours very affectionately,

Vera

PS What's all this about being a bigamist?

PPS I think we'll leave Audrey's stories of Clive until you are feeling stronger.

4 November

Dear Vera,

Thank you for another lovely letter. When you said you used to be known as 'Vee', it struck a big chord, and I wonder if your maiden named used to be Day? I certainly remember very strongly feeling a great affection for a couple of people (have you a sister?) called V E Day and V J Day. I can't think why I didn't know them by their Christian names.

My recovery is going apace. I got my hearing back before leaving hospital, which I can't say has been much of a comfort, since the only people who have been speaking to me are that awful girl, Lesley; my solicitor, who keeps saying, 'That'll be another hundred pounds please'; and the police, and the conversations have been rather one-sided. However, a few days ago when I was out shopping for a couple of chops for the barbecue (barbecues for one are fun – the dinner lasts longer, you feel it's an occasion, there's less washing up, and there's nobody to see the bits of charcoal round your mouth), a young man grabbed me by the collar, shoved a water pistol in my face, and said if I didn't give him my pension and my jewellery, I'd be dead. Before I knew what I was doing, I'd stamped on his instep, elbowed him in the solar plexus and, picking him up off the floor, had hissed, 'Stealing from the elderly shrinks your goolies, you worthless haemorrhoid.' I don't know who was more surprised, him or me. I didn't dare make a citizen's arrest and march him to the police station in case they tried to get me on another assault charge, but I can tell you I was rather pleased with myself and have been walking taller ever since. But imagine those being my first words! I went straight back home and tried practising in front of the mirror, but so far all I can seem to manage are rude words, which is why I haven't phoned you – I'd hate

you to get the wrong idea. I'm persevering, and so long as
I have at least one swear word in the sentence, I seem to
be able to manage. This morning I asked the milkman to
leave half a pint of bastard cream! The strange thing is, I
don't seem to care about the impression I make now, and
in a way I'll be sorry if that wears off.

In the meantime, I've been fascinated by my apparent
bigamy and have been spending a lot of time staring at the
two wedding photos, hoping it might jog my memory, but
so far all I'm getting are impressions. There is the one of
me with the man who was called Clive, and to be honest
I'm not much drawn to him at all. He looks a self-satisfied
bugger (heavens, I hope my foul mouth isn't going to get
the better of my letter writing!), and from this vantage
point I can't honestly think what I saw in him. I am not
filled with love or tenderness when I look at him, more
irritation and a vague memory of unacceptable bodily
functions. But the other man! Well, I feel hot and cold,
trembly knee-ed, that I'd do anything for him, anything. I
hear his voice, I see him with his arm around me, holding
me fast, saying in a strong clear voice, 'You and me, my
darling, together, always, now and across the unknown
aeons. Never leave me, for I should be lost entirely.' And I
obviously did, and now he is. What can I have been
thinking of? I feel very strongly that if only I could track
him down I would know true happiness to the end of my
days – but then again, I feel curiously contented now.
Maybe I should have had a blow to the head years ago – I
feel unconstrained, as if I've finally managed to get to the
powder room and take off a crippling corset. Some days I
wake up and think, I really should do that dusting, and
then I think, sod that for a game of soldiers, and I go to the
library instead, or go swimming. Last night I went to the
pictures on my own and had a bag of popcorn and a hot
dog and thoroughly enjoyed myself. The girl looked at me
a bit askance when I gave her my money and asked for

one to see *Rain Bollocks*, but what do I care? If that boy
Dustin Hoffman can get work with his appalling
disabilities, then I can certainly pay my way to watch him
at it.

If you feel like taking a real risk, I'd quite fancy an
outing with you in the not-too-distant. What do you say –
shall we go and paint the town red – or blue in my case?
Could you cope? Write and let me know soon. I've got to
go now as there's a man at the door wanting to read the
frigging meter.

Lots of love,

Irene

7 November

My very dear Irene,

I've been casting around in my mind for an occasion it might be appropriate to take you to with your current affliction. The WI Autumn Fayre hardly seems it. I don't think our chairwoman would take kindly to abusive name-calling (though goodness knows I've often been tempted), nor does the vicarage Bonfire Party appeal, though the vicar, of course, is quite used to it.

I think I might have hit upon the solution, though. Our local Am-Dram society is about to give their seasonal treat at the Astor Arts and Crafts Centre, so how about coming to that? So much language flies about between these theatrical types, that if you called one of them a 'silly old bugger' to their face, I doubt they would even notice. They are a gay crowd and their first nights are notoriously pleasant. Everyone gets squiffy in the bar before and after (and on one occasion, during, if King Lear's hiccups were anything to go by) and there's always a party at one or other of their houses. To be honest, I've never been, though I've once or twice been invited.

Gerald couldn't abide that crowd, which he always referred to as 'the suede-shoe brigade'. The only time I managed to get him to a show (that thing about two tramps – very boring) he fell asleep and snored loudly. Was my face red! Gordon Scarth, the president of our Antiques and Collectables Club, had 'directed' it and he was sitting right next to me. I plied him with gin and tonics later and blamed it all on Gerald's hayfever. Speaking of which, that is the name of the piece the Astor players are giving. I believe it's very light – not at all 'arty' – so I don't think it will tax what's left of your poor old grey matter. It opens on the Thursday, so why not come that afternoon and stay for the rest of the weekend? I'll think of some other place we can visit without giving offence. I can't wait to try you on the 49 bus driver – do you know any Caribbean obscenities?

This business about a blow to the head is very intriguing. *I* was hit by a flying brick during an air-raid. I was concussed for a week and afterwards married Gerald. Now you've started me wondering . . .

Till next week, my dear,

With all love,

Vera

Grossthorpe Police Cells

18 November

Dear Vera,

As you can see from the above address, I am in dire straits and beg you to help. When I got off the train at Grossthorpe coming back from you, I went to get my car from the station car park and bumped into Bruce, who was about to get his train to Cynnington to take up his new duties. A few parishioners were with him to see him off – Beryl Mainwaring, who you met at the Ladies Night, Judith Brain and Marjorie Bostock. After we'd put him on the train and waved it out of sight, we decided to go and have a coffee in Grey's Coffee Lounge, but as we were walking down the High Street, Veronica St John spotted us and came over for a chat. All these girls, except Judith, had been on the demonstration, and they were asking me how I was and how I'd felt about being charged. We were all filling Judith in and getting quite heated, and the next thing I know, I'm being bundled into a police car, charged under the Public Order Act. Apparently you aren't allowed to talk to more than one person at a time in the street these days, otherwise it's a political meeting or you're inciting them to riot or something. Of course, my swearing affliction didn't help – the girls found it quite amusing, and were copying me, so I suppose we were getting a bit out of hand – and you can imagine my surprised response to the two young officers who arrested me. Or rather, I hope you can't, as I believe I surpassed myself this time. My solicitor has read it to me, blushing crimson all the time, as they had written it all down in their notebooks to use as evidence against me.

This morning I was remanded in custody awaiting trial, which could be for anything up to two years apparently, owing to the queues. I am beside myself about Sidney. He's already been in kennels for ages while I was in hospital, and I'd put him in again at the weekend when I was visiting you. I'm sure he'll pine and die before I get out. Would you, could you, please get him for me and look after him until my return? I know it's a big favour to ask – indeed, if things go against me, it could be a lifetime's job – but you are the only person I have ever seen him register affection with beside myself. He even used to go for Clive, and for a giant poodle, that's quite rare. He is at Pampered Pets Holiday Homes, Little Throssle 634. Forgive me for asking, but it's just one thing too many for me to worry about at the moment.

Apart from all this, I had a thoroughly enjoyable weekend with you, notwithstanding the drama at the play. I'm so sorry my memory had to return all in a rush like that during the quiet scene in the second act, but as I already explained to you, it was seeing that girl 'dry up' and hearing her 'prompt' called from the wings that sped me back in time to my first 'marriage'. It's nice to know I'm not a bigamist, but sad to think that he who I had come to think of as the great love of my life had only been Cyril Organ acting out his part in the title role of *The Errant Spouse*. I hope you weren't too embarrassed afterwards. I must say, they were very decent about it in the bar.

Conditions here aren't too bad, except that they're too overcrowded to allow visits at the moment. I am sharing my cell with two very nice girls and their mother, who are all charged with murdering a rapist while in the course of his duties. How the other half live! My spirits have risen since a kind WPC showed me yesterday's *Mercury* – Marjorie Bostock and the girls are organising an 'Irene Spencer Is Innocent' Bring and Buy to try to raise my bail. I hope it's a good turn-out, as it's been set at a quarter of a million pounds.

Please write when you can. My solicitor is going to smuggle this out for me and post it on to you, as apparently the censoring is awful. Yesterday, my cell mates received a letter, 'Dear Aunty Doris and Girls, ████████ ████████ ████████ ████████ ████████ ████████ ████████ ████████ ████████ ████████████ All the best, Tracie Louise'.

Hope you are keeping well. Sorry to be a bother.

Lots of love,

Irene

PS Sidney hates tinned food of any kind except for salmon.

PPS Irene Spencer is innocent!

26th ██████

My ██████ Irene,

This is ████████████! What ██████s those ████████████s must have been to ████████ you, even if you did call them ████ing ████████ ████████ ████████s (your solicitor rang me). I'm beginning to believe what Karen says about them; before I'd always put it down to ████████-wing paranoia? As for this ████████ing business, we shall just have to talk in code like ████████sof war, shan't we?

Don't worry about Sidney, I've collected him and I must say he *was* glad to see me. I didn't have any salmon handy, so I gave him a tin of snails Howard bought on his last duty-free trip and, do you know, he wolfed them! I think my arms have grown a foot since we've been going 'walkies'.

I've been in touch with ████████████ about the ████████ and ████████ ████████████ and I'm mustering everyone able from here. The Great Potterton Players have really entered into the spirit and are going to mount a special show. I think it's *Oh! Calcutta!*.

One word of advice – be careful who you fall in with there. Karen was taken to ████████ once after a demo and the things she saw – unnatural acts using ████████s, and ████████s, and that was only the warders!

Must go, Sidney is barking.

All my ████████

Vera

Cell 4
Grossthorpe Police Station
4 December

Dear Vera,

Don't send your letters direct to the above address – I
could hardly decipher a word of your last, so full of blanks
was it. And anyway, I've heard on the grapevine that I'm
to be moved soon, I'm not sure where. Write c/o my
solicitors, Crabbe, Sidebottom and Partners, 5 Dresden
Street, Grossthorpe, and Mr Ricketts will smuggle it to me,
wherever I am. Apparently he is going to give my briefs to
a lady barrister, which is what I call progress! He says she
is the best I can afford, as she is young and black and only
a woman, but I think he's jealous that he never got to wear
a wig and gown himself. (That looks rather queer written
down, doesn't it?)

The days go slowly in here, and even though I can't
quite get the meaning of your missive, I read it every night
and sleep with it under my pillow. Another girl joined us
in our cell yesterday, so now we are five. I must say she
paints a very attractive picture of prison proper, and I shall
almost be disappointed if I don't get 'sent down' (excuse
my criminal jargon). She defaulted on her mortgage
payments, got 'banged up' for four years and came out
with a degree in Economics. Now she's got into trouble
with her credit cards, on purpose, so she can gain her PhD.
She couldn't get a grant for it on the outside.

The kind WPC came into the cell last night just before
lights out, removed her tunic, unbuttoned her shirt, and
stuck her chest out at me. Underneath she was wearing a
FREE IRENE SPENCER T-shirt. Judith Brain's husband got his
students to print them at the Polytechnic where he works.
I feel quite a celebrity! Brenda (the WPC) tells me they're
selling like hot cakes, which is good, as the proceeds are to

go towards my trial costs (I think they've abandoned trying to raise the quarter of a million for my bail), but that she herself had been given hers by a working girl as a bribe for not 'running her in'. These are certainly treacherous times we are living in, if even a typist has to bribe the police not to arrest her.

Anyway, must sign off now as I've used up all this paper – sorry about the Bronco, but they're very stingy here with the stationery. It'll be Christmas soon, and I won't be able to send any cards. But then again, it'll be nice to have company. I *wish* you could visit me. Brace up, Irene. No sniffles. *Non, je ne regret rien.*

Fondest love,

Prisoner F5138

PS Thank you so much for rescuing Sidney – you are a friend indeed. I hope he is 'behaving' himself, and that your arms will soon adjust to his strength. Give him a kiss and tell him Mummy loves him.

My dear Irene,

I've always wanted to visit one of Her Majesty's residences but would have preferred it to have been Buckingham Palace. This sojourn has nothing to do with voluntary work, nor indeed voluntary anything, and the food is abominable. I can only hope the Queen's personal cooks are of a more regal standard. Two days after I sent off your last letter Customs and Excise dropped in. Through the skylight. Others entered by the more regular route of the front door, but as this was locked and bolted at the time (4.15 a.m.) they left rather a large hole, having axed down three of the panels. Really, lager louts cause less damage!

Apparently they suspect me of being an international Drug Runner, but this I only learned after they had smashed my entire collection of Port Merion teapots and ripped up all the upholstery. I was 'gobsmacked', to use one of Karen's favourite phrases, quite literally, as I had a tea towel shoved in my mouth, I suppose to stop me screaming. When I'd recovered enough to speak, they demanded to know 'who or what was "Sidney" '. I should have thought that was self-evident as the poor lamb was shut in the kitchen, howling more ear-shatteringly than the Hound of the Baskervilles, but they persisted in thinking he was a euphonism for drug abuse, as is 'going walkies'. 'Salmon' is 'crack', 'snails' a type of psychedelic substance which makes you feel like a giant. It's all because I made a reference to talking in code in your letter. Speaking of which, I shall think twice next time I hear my Irish librarian say she had 'great crack' at the weekend!

This is being smuggled out for me by a charming Jamaican girl with whom I've been sharing a cell. She's going 'on parole' today, and thinks she may stay out long enough to post a letter. I haven't been allowed to see a lawyer until I 'confess', but I have had a visit from Karen, who has taken Sidney though how she will manage I don't know. She is hugely pregnant with swollen ankles and the baby is still two months off. I asked her if twins run in her ex-paramour's family. She said shortly that she had no idea if he even had a family and the only sort of twins he'd mentioned were carburettors. Try as I might, I can't picture that relationship.

Well, my dear, I must close as Maxine has her running shoes on and is eager to be off. I don't know how long they can hold me without a charge. Karen says about a year, she thinks, so who knows, you might be getting a visit from me sooner than expected!

Keep your pecker up.

Love,

Vee

PS Can't bear to think what they're going to serve up for Christmas dinner. But, look on the bright side, Irene, it's an easy way to diet!

Cell 214
HM Prison Ship *Pride of Cleveland*

20 December

My dear Vee,

What a chapter of incidence and coincidence! I have just
heard on the grapevine that you and I are in the same
boat, so to speak. Maxine was picked up almost
immediately for possession of an offensive weapon (her
Afro comb) and was very upset not to have had time to
post your letter. Imagine her surprise when she found she
was sharing a cell with me! I'd just read your letter, and
she was telling me how you'd been keeping their spirits
up with songs from the Blitz and your impressions of the
warders, when we were bundled up with our few
possessions and shipped out here. Something about
clearing the on-shore cells to cope with the anticipated
rush of arrests following the amendment to the blasphemy
laws – have you heard the same rumour on your deck?

News of your famous impersonations have reached our
ears down here on Deck F – you are awful, I bet the
Governor never said anything *like* that! – and Maxine said,
'It's got to be Vera!', and our contact said yes, she believed
that was the name. We'd been hoarding a wine gum for
some special celebration, and the six of us in here were all
of one mind, to toast Vera! We each had a nibble, and
honestly felt quite intoxicated afterwards, but I imagine
that was more, due to High 'Spirits'!!

Listen, my dear friend, rest assured that you won't be in
for much longer. I have made a deposition to my lawyer –
well, at least, I will have when I'm allowed to send it –
stating your innocence re your connection with a drugs
ring. I've written it all down on Bronco, but so far I haven't
been able to post it due to staff shortages – apparently

they're all calling in sick at the moment as they want to spend Christmas with their families. Don't we all?! Well, no, actually, in my case, although I'd give anything to be the one to mince Sidney's giblets for him on The Big Day.

Hope you can read this – isn't it amazing how small you can make your writing when you've only got the one sheet? Tomorrow I shall try to save two so we can have a really good chin-wag. I'm now going to give this to Janice, who's on kitchen duties, so she can give it to the girl on your deck. It's very pleasant, this feeling of comradeship, isn't it? No wonder they go on about the Brotherhood of Man. Seems silly that it's taken prison to introduce me to the Sisterhood of Women.

Oh well, so much for waxing philosophical. All for now, my dear. Keep your spirits up.

All love,

Irene X

24 December

Dearest Irene,

The rumour *we* heard was that the police were expecting a post-Xmas deluge of wife beaters, rampaging champagne louts and down-and-outs back on the streets after stints as Father Christmas. I must say your version is much more interesting and explains why a warder told me to turn round three times and spit when I mentioned Mrs Thatcher. Has she been deified? Perhaps the Pope has made an unscheduled ground-kissing visit to Chequers while we've been 'inside'. Karen will be pleased – she told me long ago the Monarchy should be abolished. Speaking of Karen, I had a (censored) note from her on Friday. ████████ is in the best of health, though his barks are annoying the neighbours.

I'm delighted news of my 'cabarets' is reaching 'F' Deck. It *is* amazing what prison brings out in you. Of course, I always knew I was a performer. When I was a toddler my father's favourite trick was to tell me to go to the door and 'fetch it'. I'd get down on all fours and crawl to him with the paper. I've had prisoners and warders alike in tucks with my snatches of *Guys and Dolls*. We're a bit short of 'guys' of course, but you'd be surprised what you can do with Sellotape and brown paper! I've made some very supportive friends. I completely agree with you about the 'Sisterhood', but I can't believe this is what Karen means. She never has a good word for any of her friends and is always enraged at their writing. I wonder what she'd think if she could read our correspondence? Probably that, like ████████, we are 'barking'.

I believe tomorrow we may meet, as due to staff shortages we're all to be herded together for our turkey roll and Smash potatoes. We're to be allowed to watch the Queen's speech, before being given our Librium.

Well, my dear, all for now as I am hanging up my stocking (hand-knitted by a lady at 'Release') and joining my cell-mates in a few heart-warming carols. I will think of you as I sing. A very Merry Christmas, my friend, and may we be able to greet the New Year free in Spirit, if not in body.

Your own Vera

Solitary Cell C
Christmas Day

My dearest, dearest Vee,

How *good* it was to see you today, and to be lucky enough to sit next to you during the Queen! Never has human contact ever meant so much to me. Sitting there in the dark, save for the flickering illumination of Her Majesty, holding your hand – it's the best Christmas present I could ever wish for. Forgive me for weeping so foolishly. It was just that, being so near you, it put me in mind of all the happy times we've shared on the 'outside' – and the heartache. It's true what they say, isn't it – you don't know what you've got till it's gone.

What a wonderful idea of yours to swap socks for our Christmas presents to each other. Now all I need do when I'm blue and missing you is to look at my feet! You are a dear.

Please don't be upset about me being caught talking to you. I honestly don't mind the thought of solitary now that I've seen you, and it's only for five days. My greatest hope is that I can behave myself well enough for them to honour their promise and let me out in time for the so-called New Year 'celebrations', so I might have the chance to see you again. I have found a small hole round a pipe that runs through this cell, and have ascertained that it goes right through to the cell above, by whispering and knocking. A nice woman called Susan, who is in for writing rude words on her water shares application, says that she'll smuggle this note to you if I push it up to her. Do you know her? She sounded as if she knew you, but then, as we know, your celebrity runs before you!

Vee, when we get out of here (note I don't say if!), shall we set up house together? Being in here, despite the bad things, I *have* enjoyed the company. I don't think I could bear to go back to my lonely house in Hethergreen after this, by myself. If we teamed up, we could sell one or both of our houses, pool our resources and live the life of Riley. We could even have Karen and the baby to stay with us at first, if she has nowhere else to go. Only two months to go before the birth of her first, and no mother to lean on – she must be going frantic.

What I was trying to tell you when I got caught is that I've had a letter from Lesley. It was so nasty, they'd left it completely uncensored – I suppose it's only the nice, supportive, friendly things they cut out, the devils. In it, she told me that word had spread to Wollongong about my 'evil deeds', and that after a 'family conference' with Keith, they have decided to cut me out of their will! As if that matters to me! It's true that since she's shown her true colours, I've often wished her dead, but not for any financial advantage to me. Anyway, that's as nothing to the rest. They have told my little Cheryl Marie that Nanna has gone to Heaven. How could they? Lesley says it is to save her from the stigma of having a convict for a relative, but I'd have thought that in Australia, *not* having one in the family would stigmatise you even more. Anyway, I'm not going to let it upset me – I've got enough on my hands – and if necessary I'll just have to wait until Cheryl Marie is old enough to open her own mail, before I can let her know the good news that I'm alive – and well.

You may be surprised at the length of this letter, but the one advantage of being in solitary is not having to share the Bronco! I could go on for a whole roll, but I must keep this thin enough to push through the hole to Susan.

The warder just came in to give me my night medication, so I'll have to sign off now as I can already feel myself nodding off. Happy Boxing Day, my dear. I shall think of you over the turkey goulash. I'm going to wear my socks in bed tonight, as a special holiday treat.

They can't take *that* away from me! My feet in your socks, my hand in yours. What a day!

All love and seasons greetings,

Irene xx

29 December

Dear Irene,

I was rather troubled when I received your last. Frankly you sound unhinged in it. 'My feet in your socks, your hand in mine'! What is this? Some kind of suicide love pact?! Do be careful, my dear. Surrounded as we are by censoring eyes and ears, you don't want to say things that give the wrong impression! (Susan, by the way, works in the sewer block with me. She's working class, though a well-meaning soul. She fancies herself as an artist and has done colourful 'primitives' on her cell wall. The Authorities won't provide her with paints, so she's made use of bodily functions.)

Thank you for your lovely extra present – a papier-mâché toothmug is just what I've always wanted. Did you chew up all that Bronco yourself? What a labour of love. I managed to smuggle out a Christmas token to Howard (a crust of bread with my teethmarks in it) and yesterday I was allowed a visit from him. He brought me a belated Christmas gift (a goatskin smock and half a pound of muesli) and an admission. He is 'gay'. He said I wasn't to worry, he and Antony are thoroughly monogamous and they've both been HIV-tested. I said that reassuring as that was, it wouldn't help with the neighbours. He said he was very sorry, he knew I'd be upset, but he couldn't live a lie any longer, he was sick of 'being in the closet'. The word 'closet' put me in mind of that Masonic business of Gerald's I found. Again, I can't help wondering . . .

I can't deny it is a momentous shock, though, if I'm honest, I knew there was 'something'. I blame my mother, who had knitted him pink. People were always stopping by his pram to say, 'Who's a lovely girl then?' I cried all night at the thought of my lost grandchildren. But today, my cell-mate Beefy (an ex-Hell's Angel) has given me a heart-to-heart on people of 'the other persuasion'. Apparently they are not as I'd supposed, plain and unattractive, but can be quite normal, just like us. They have dogs and are kind to old people. I can't say I'm completely reconciled, but Beefy has promised that if I cheer up she'll do a tattoo on my navel.

Howard said that Karen's had a nasty bout of flu. The hospital have told her she'll have to have a home birth as they've got no beds. I do so wish I could be with her.

Vee

PS Only a couple of days to go before you are back among us!

Cell 214

1 January

Dear Vera,

A pinch and a punch for the first day of the month, and quite frankly, a good kick in the behind for being so rude in your last. 'Unhinged'? You try being in solitary in the bowels of a ship with no heating in a force 8 gale, then let's talk about 'unhinged'! In those conditions you cling to the happy memories of warm friendship, or what you had been led to believe was warm friendship, anyway. I suppose you'll be accusing me of coming out of the cupboard next, or whatever you call it. As for Howard – how could you have been so blind? I tried to tell you once, but you refused to hear me. And so what, if they love each other? You're so prejudiced and narrow-minded sometimes, a thing that Karen has often pointed out to me that I am not. And I know another thing that you're going to have to swallow in the not-too-distant, so I just hope that your experiences in here will have made you more tolerant and a bit less anxious to condemn.

They let me out of solitary yesterday, so I was at the New Year's Eve celebration and saw you making a fool of yourself with who I can only assume is she who is known as 'Beefy'. Who wants a mermaid tattooed round their navel? You'll have to live with that for the rest of your life. Everybody in my cell thinks that you've gone stir-crazy. I didn't come over and say hello, as you seemed to be having a whale of a time without me. My mother always warned me about people who transfer their affections easily, but I have never learned. The girls in my cell say it is because of my low self-esteem, and they are trying to raise my conscience about it each day after slop-out.

My good news, if you're interested, is that the lady

barrister has prepared my briefs and we are taking them
before the Court quite soon. *They* won't tell me when, but
they say I'll know when I am blindfolded in a dinghy,
being rowed ashore. I just wish I was a better sailor – I feel
queasy at the thought.

Not one to bear malice, I wish you a Happy New Year
among your new friends.

With all good wishes for your future,

Irene

Prisoner 290001
Cell Block H

Wensdy

Deer Ireen,

Vee has arsked me to write this four her as she is
indisposd dew to a nastee bowt of blood poisnin. I had
simlar with my 'Satan livs' tattoo, but that was dun with a
pin. She is verry sory you hav taken agenst her and wants
to make it up beefour she dise? diys? dyes, which is onlee
to likeley as I dun hers with a fork.

She sends orl her luv and hops yor breefs will be easy.

Yrs faithfullee

Beefy

PS Her dorter went into prematur laber last nite but
hasunt had a result yet.

12 January

'Dear' Beefy,

At last I am free. Say goodbye to Vera for me. I am in the dinghy, afloat on the great sea of life, and apart from the biliousness, I feel very optimistic. My trial begins tomorrow. I shall win.

It is such a comfort to know that Vera is in your hands, and off mine. She is such a responsibility and has quite a vicious temper. Furthermore she is selfish, egotistical, vain, and not a fit mother. I shall be taking care of Karen and her baby on my release, as that is what she wants. It will be better if Vera stays away from us, as we shall have our hands full of nappies, and will be able to do without having to minister to the needs of her second childhood. The baby's father is a West Indian, by the way. Break the news to Vera as brutally as you like.

All good wishes for a wonderful life in prison together.

Yours,

Irene Spencer,
An innocent and soon-to-be free woman

HM Prison Ship *Pride of Cleveland*

21 April

Dear Mrs Spencer,

I am so very pleased your trial has gone smoothly and your days of captivity are over. Careful not to fall behind with the poll tax, or we shall be seeing you back again. Ha! Ha! Yes, everyone here gave a very big cheer when they heard of your acquittal on the grounds of diminished responsibility. Everyone, that is, except poor Vera Small, who has passed into what appears to be a terminal coma and has not murmured a word since your last was read out to her. On removal to the hospital wing, she was thought to sigh, 'Oh, Irene . . .' but her friend Beefy insisted it was merely the air escaping from her catheter. Beefy has indeed been a devoted nurse, running herself ragged to fulfil all Vera's (unspoken) needs. Never have I witnessed so much energy expended for so little return; at this rate Beefy will shortly be hospitalised also. I don't know what denomination you follow, or indeed if your experiences here have rendered you totally Godless, but can I, as a man of faith, beg you to send one word of forgiveness? You may have had a serious falling-out with Vera, but I cannot believe you wish her dead, or at least, not without your blessing. Your solicitors tell me you are selling your house and moving away. I fervently pray this reaches you before you commit the irrevocable.

God bless,

Rev. Trev (prison chaplain)

PS Vera has a granddaughter, as I expect you know. Her daughter has made several attempts to bring her out of the coma by dangling the baby in front of her face. She explained to Beefy it was 'shock' therapy, but so far never a flicker.

The Vicarage
Cynnington

27 April

Dear Trev,

How *are* you, you old son of a gun? I couldn't believe it
when Irene Spencer passed me your letter. I'd no idea you
were working on a prison ship these days. *Bonjour, matelot!*
I, for my sins, have recently taken over the parish of St
Cuthbert the Untainted, and am having a whale of a time
judging marrows and eating seed cake. Come over and see
me some time when you get shore leave, and we'll finish
that debate about the Ascension that we never quite
resolved at the Varsity. Have you heard from Chris and
Jumbo recently? I had a postcard from them at Christmas –
they really are a scream.

I'm sorry to hear about Vera Smalls. Mrs Spencer, an ex-
parishioner of mine, is alarmed to hear of her imminent
death and has asked me to write, sending her blessing. At
the moment she has her hands pretty full as she is looking
after Vera's daughter Karen and her new-born baby, and is
organising a 'Vera Smalls Is Innocent' Fork and Finger
Buffet. She has asked me to ask you to ask Vera for the
recipe for the Blue Cheese Dip. You may have read in the
papers about her sensational trial, but if not I enclose a
cutting. Read it to Vera and see if you get a flicker.
Apparently it's crucial that you do, as the Blue Cheese Dip
is central to the theme of the Buffet. Irene also suggests
that you shout, 'Beef up, Vera', very loudly in her left ear
(she's a bit Mutt and Jeff in her right).

Hope you can bring it off. Shall I buy you a ticket to the
bunfight? Irene's cooking is quite legendary. Tell Vera that
Howard will be there – he's her number-one son, and a
great friend of mine. Irene and Karen are staying with him

in the Derby Dales at the moment, so send the recipe care of him, Sheepdipper's Shed, Shooters Hill, Shale, Shap, Nr Great Shagthorne, Derbs. And write to me soon, you old reprobate!

Yours ever, in love and peace, sickness and health,

Bruce Springthorpe

The Daily Satellite, 12 April

SEX-MAD GRANNY IS LOCO, SAYS JUDGE

Hundreds of ex-prisoners, OAPs, ethnic minorities and peace loonies cheered in court yesterday when diminutive Irene Spencer was officially declared mad and set free.

In his address to the court at the end of the trial, Judge Branston Pickles said that her voluntary sterilisation had tipped the balance in her favour, and that he was returning her to the community 'for better or worse'.

Asked for her comments outside the Old Bailey, buxom Irene (85) read from a sheet of Bronco which she had prepared earlier, stating the innocence of her 'friend' Vera Smalls (96).

Vera, still serving time for drugs running, is currently in a coma on a prison ship off the British Isles and official sources say that she is 'very poorly'.

Close friends and relatives are preparing themselves for the worst, but Irene, who claims she is neither, is battling on to free her. 'If they think I'm mad,' says Irene, 'they should meet Vera. She is completely barking, and should he released.'

HM Prison Ship *Pride of Cleveland*

3 May

Brucie baby!

How fabby-dabby to hear from you. Chris and Jumbo told me you were dead. Something about a contaminated jab when you were out in the Tropics. They're so pleased to know it was a false alarm, or rather they will be in six months when they get my letter. They are currently up the Orinoco, camping with Pongo and Gerry.

Well, well, you old rugger-bugger, reading your letter brought it all back. Great times eh? D'you still keep up with your sport? Hope all that cake isn't sending you to seed! I'm still rowing. As you can imagine, in my present billet it's nothing short of essential. I've got an arrangement with a jolly tar – we take it in turns in the dinghy! I'd love to come and see you. I get leave twice a year (more if I threaten to expose the horrors of shipboard life . . . I've got a nice one up my cassock about the governor and the stoker) so I'll pop along to the Fork and Finger. Meanwhile I enclose a missive from Vera Small, who has made a miraculous recovery. I'd like to think it was the laying on of hands that did it, but Vera insists her friend Beefy had been doing that for weeks to no avail, so it must have been the cutting. Certainly, when I shouted 'Vera Small . . . 96' in her left ear a strange seizure overcame her. She's now back to normal, or as normal as I gather she ever is – spends all day pacing her cell and ranting at poor Beefy who has lost a stone and was yesterday found dangling from a porthole.

Yours in Christ, till we meet again,

Your ever loving,

Trevor

TO WHOM IT MAY CONCERN

Vera Small wishes it to be known that she entirely dissociates herself from anything said or done by Irene Spencer in the so-called 'Vera Small Is Innocent' campaign. As for the blue cheese dip, the recipe is a family secret, though not one, you may be sure, that has been, or ever will be, passed on to her ungrateful children.

She would like to remind certain persons whom it is that stood collateral for the mortgage on Sheep Shagger's Bottom or whatever it's called and indeed who has paid the gas and electricity for the last two quarters, not to mention settling a bill for outstanding rent with her beggarly daughter's landlord. She is in touch with her solicitor about her will, so let them put that in their pipes and smoke it whilst thinking of her lying in this stinking hold. And no, I am not referring to the embraces of Beefy, whose personal hygiene has improved immensely since sharing a cell with a civilising influence and whose affection is not, unlike that of some others, in question. She may be rough but she is always more than ready.

Vera is currently fully engaged in teaching Beefy to read and write and will shortly be starting her own campaign to bring literacy to Her Majesty's prisons. She is sure she will find joy in contributing to the wider good and thus recover from the terrible hurt done her by her family and 'friends', who cannot, it seems, be bothered to write her a letter!

Sheepdipper's Shed

8 May

Darling Mummy,

Bruce Springthorpe has just given us your To Whom It May Concern, and we're all terribly upset. How can you have got it so wrong? We all love you desperately, and are literally working night and day to get you out of that terrible place. I couldn't bear seeing you there at Christmas – I'm not ashamed to say that I wept for days afterwards. Irene has been an inspiration to us all, never giving up, battling on through thick and thin, always confident that Right will triumph. She has even made bold attempts to get Beefy released too so that you can be together when you get out, and honestly, I don't think there is a greater love than that.

Darling Mums, please let us help you. Irene knows what she's doing. You have to be mad to get out of prison these days, it's the only way. Please trust us and play along. We're having a big fund-raising party for you in a couple of days, and we're hoping to get lots of publicity. Nigel Norris of the *Shagthorne Gazette* has given a definite yes, but we're still working on Jimmy Young.

I wish you could be with us, Mummy. We all miss you and talk about you all the time. Come home to us. All you have to do is roll your eyes and slobber a bit – is that too much to ask?

Eat this when you've finished reading it. It's on organic brown rice paper which I've impregnated with Gentian Flower Remedy – it'll cheer you up.

```
XXXXXXXXXX                    XXXXXXXX
 XXXXXXX     All my love,     XXXXXXX
  XXXXXX                       XXXXXX
   XXXX                         XXXX
    XX                           XX
     X          Howie             X
```

Sheepdipper's Shed

8 May

My dear Vera,

Please be nice and come out of prison. Poor darling Howard is going off his head, and the worry is undoing all the good work he did on himself in the Flotation Tank last year. I'm sorry that you think it's so dreadful that I love your son and that he loves me. Personally, I can't think of anything nicer. Except for both of us to have your love too.

This funny-looking note-paper is organically farmed seaweed which I've smeared with Royal Jelly – that's what the Queen takes, and look how marvellous she is. In fact, I know several old queens who do very well on it indeed! Oh dear, camp joke, whoopsee. Hope you've still got your sense of humour.

Oh well, I'd better drag myself up and get back in the kitchen – there's still acres of pastry to roll out for your party.

Till we meet again, lots of love, ducks, and a big kiss.

Antony x

c/o Sheepdipper's Shed

8 May

Mum

For Christ's sake stop being pig-headed, grow up, and get your arse in gear. It's horrible here with everybody weeping and wailing all the time, and I'm sick to the back teeth of your usual ingratitude. We're all killing ourselves for you, as per, and all we get is insults.

Do you remember when I climbed the plum tree when I was six because you'd been foul to me, and I got stuck? When Dad wanted to call the Fire Brigade you just said, 'No, leave her, it'll teach her a lesson. She'll come down when she's cold and hungry. Either that or she'll *fall* out eventually'? That's pretty much the way I feel about you right now. The others, of course, being soppy, are trying to put a ladder up to you, which you keep kicking, but if Howard loses any more weight over this he'll be dead within a month.

Stop being so frigging selfish. Got to go – Sabrina's just puked down my neck.

Karen

The Vicarage
Cynnington

Dear Trev,

Enc. some missives for Vera Smalls from her family and friends – thought I'd send them post-haste, even though I'll be seeing you in a couple of days. We're going ahead with the beanfeast despite her dissociating herself from it, and just pray that she will see the light.

Fancy Pongo and Gerry still being together after all that falling out over the Transubstantiation! If only all Holy Wars could be so happily resolved!!

I'm encing a small notette from me to Mrs Smalls, too. I've heard the grub in there is pretty grot, so I've written it on (unsanctified) communion wafers. Tell her to pig the lot when she's read it.

Can't wait till Saturday. Sunday Mrs Wiggins is going to do us lamb *en croûte*, so as soon as I get the silly old services out of the way, we can tuck in and get stinko like the good old days. Should more than make up for the load of old lentils we'll get at Sheepdipper's at the bash. For afters I've asked for Grand Marnier soufflé, her absolute speciality. Why the hell shouldn't we clergy enjoy ourselves? Tee hee, aren't I naughty? I've just been doing my parish rounds, and I've had a couple of sherries over the eight.

Peace and love,

Brucie baby

1. The Vicarage Cynnington
   8 May
   Dear Mrs Small,

   PTO

I've written this on
communion wafers which,

please turn to next . . .

2. means I can't get
   much on to a page but

   PTO

at least you'll have a square
(or round, ha ha) meal

please turn to next . . .

3. out of it. Your
   friends and family

   PTO

all love and miss you
and want more

please turn to next . . .

4. than anything to
   help you come out

   PTO

of prison. Being
insane is

please turn to next . . .

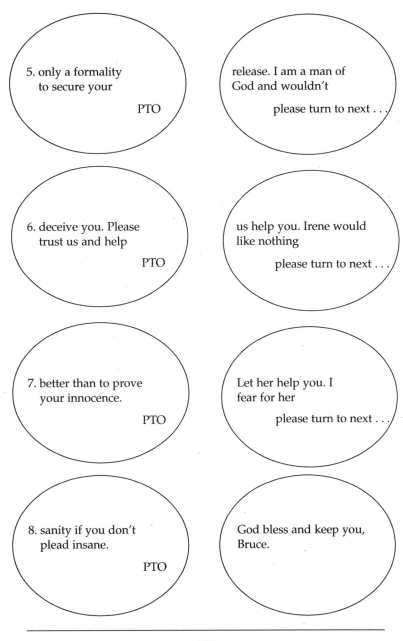

5. only a formality
to secure your

PTO

release. I am a man of
God and wouldn't

please turn to next . . .

6. deceive you. Please
trust us and help

PTO

us help you. Irene would
like nothing

please turn to next . . .

7. better than to prove
your innocence.

PTO

Let her help you. I
fear for her

please turn to next . . .

8. sanity if you don't
plead insane.

PTO

God bless and keep you,
Bruce.

c/o Sheepdipper's Shed

10 May

Dear Vera,

I don't know what right you've got to get shirty with me, but we'll let that pass. If you're cross about your age in the paper, how do you think I felt about being called a buxom eighty-five? If you're cross about me saying you're insane, you must be mad. *I* am perfectly compos, but I wasn't too proud to be declared unsound of mind if that meant my liberty. Doing this literacy course is all very nice, but I don't think it'll help our case much – nor does my lady barrister, who I've hired to examine your briefs, and which she's been doing in detail since last Monday week. She's also trying to get Beefy an appeal, so has been going through her briefs as well. I can't begin to tell you what she's found there so far, but I do advise you to keep her sweet – she could turn at any moment.

I am very happy to be 'out' despite the fact that I am working my fingers to the bone. Sabrina has nappy rash and colic, Karen's eczema has flared up again, Howard is down to nine stone two, Sidney's got enteritis and Antony's long awaited ingrowing toe-nail operation was not a success. But I'll tell you this – if they all had the bubonic plague I'd sooner be here than in that hell-hole of a prison ship. See sense and be insane. I'm sending you an avocado as I remember the warders think they're foreign muck, so might actually not steal it for themselves. Hope it's not too ripe by the time you get it. Write when you can . . . What am I saying? You're the leader of the literacy course. Write soon.

Best wishes,

Irene

15 May

Dear Bruce,

Please see that all concerned get a copy of this letter. I appoint you executor of my property. Divide it as you think fit. As far as I'm concerned, you can give the lot to Oxfam.

The communion wafers were a nice thought, though they do leave one rather dry. I missed the swig of Piat d'Dor.

All the best,

Vera

PS Don't let Karen get her hands on the crystal – it would all be smashed in a fortnight.

PPS Howard's always been fond of the photo of me that stands on the bedside table.

HM Prison Ship *Pride of Cleveland*

15 May

My Dear Friends,

After eating your letters I discussed them with my
therapist (a top Harley Street man, consigned to shipboard
duties after publicly announcing the government was
barmy). He's against my declaring myself mad as,
although I am barking, it would cast aspersions on his
abilities. He says there's nothing wrong with me that
fifteen years' Freudian analysis won't put right, and as
that's at least as long as I shall be here, I might as well get
the benefit. I must say I thoroughly enjoy my sessions with
him. It's not everyone will listen while you ramble on
about yourself. My last-but-one cell-mate begged to be put
in solitary. I have relived some momentous events from
my childhood. There was the time I stuffed Teddy down
the lav and kicked my doll's house to pieces. I was
reacting against being unloved apparently, and all I can
say is I wish I'd made such a fuss in my adult life. The
times I wanted to strangle Gerald . . . now I'll never get the
opportunity. When we aren't talking about me, Arnon (my
therapist) tells me about his problems with his wife and
family. These are considerably fewer of course, with the
Bay of Biscay between them. If neither of us can think of
anything to say we ask the I Ching, which is rather
obscure for my taste, or play Scrabble, which I love, as I'm
always on the look-out to enrich my vocabulary. Arnon
got hegemony yesterday. I tried that on my literacy class
and they got very excited.

I want you all to know that I attach no blame, no, not
even to Irene, though some of the things she has said
about me are certainly less than Christian. I'm sure she is
getting her come-uppance: she's much too old to be

dealing with a baby, and as for my erstwhile family, I wish her joy of them, Arnon says they are useless baggage. Beefy's been moved to another cell. She had taken to chewing the bars with her teeth, so desperate was she to free me. But I am not entirely alone. I have planted a little seed I found in my gruel in a crack in the wall. I have nothing to feed the poor thing with, but I crumbled a bit of communion wafer on to it and watered it liberally with my tears, so hopefully God will bless it.

Goodbye, my dears. I shall try to remember the good times we had. You may never see me again but I wish you joy on your side of the great water.

Forget about me,

Vera

PS I used the avocado as a face pack, it was too far gone for consumption.

Sheepdipper's Shed

20 May

Dearest darling Mums,

Why are you doing this to me? Have you forgotten how much I love you? Why are you doing it to yourself? Oh, Mums, I've got alopecia – great scads of hair are falling out from every follicle on my body. I'm nearly bald. Mostly it happens at night, and in the morning the bed is like an animal's lair. The first morning it happened I woke up and thought that Antony was wearing a chest wig. He's being ever so sweet and supportive, but how long will it last? How can anyone love someone who looks like a boiled egg from behind? Mummy, please come and rescue me, I simply cannot bear it any longer.

The other dreadful thing is that Irene has disappeared. She said she was going underground for a while, so naturally I thought she'd gone to visit Blue John Mines, but when she didn't come back that night we all got really worried. Would she be silly enough to go pot-holing on her own? I do hope she's all right. It's ever such a strain here without her. Karen makes me and Antony babysit every night while she goes off to the pub, and she's always so *cross*.

Oh dear, dear. Two paragraphs already and I haven't said anything cheerful. Here goes. We had the Fork and Finger for your appeal and really, all things considered, it was quite a success. Jimmy Young couldn't make it in the end, as couldn't Selina Scott, Valerie Singleton, Gloria Hunniford, Terry Wogan, Esther Rantzen, Geoffrey Wainwright (MP for Shagthorne East [Con.]), Prince Charles or the Archbishop of Canterbury. However, Nigel Norris came from the *Gazette*, and because he's such a dear (he was one of the first friends I made when I moved to the area, and we were quite close for several months) he managed to rustle up Les Spatchcock to be our celebrity. You may remember that a couple of years ago Les qualified for the quarter finals of the British Snooker Contest at the Sheffield Crucible, which was televised nationwide, and for a couple of tense days the whole of Great Shagthorne held its breath. Les graciously consented to be photographed in all sorts of sporting poses for the *Gazette*, and spoke to us all on your behalf. I enclose the cutting, and hope you agree that he did a fine job to the best of his abilities. We had to guess at the Blue Cheese Dip – I sent some to you with Trevor, your prison chaplain, so you can judge for yourself the measure of our success. Personally I think there's at least one ingredient missing, but none of us could guess what it could be. Irene's roulade was its usual big hit, and I'm sending you a photograph of the celebration cake – I think Les was a bit squiffy by then!

Mums, I'm really pleased that you're having therapy and are sorting out your childhood – it took me three intensive, painful years to get over mine – but honestly there are much better facilities for that *out here*. There's a thriving alternative therapy centre right here in the village now, and I could book you a whole course of rebirthing, primal screaming, flotation, aromatherapy, reflexology and psychic healing for your birthday treat this year. Please think about it and discuss it with Arnon. Incidentally, Antony used to know an Arnon who was a therapist, but I don't imagine it was the same one. This one was struck off for the kind of unprofessional behaviour which is quite different from the sort you mentioned. Still, if it is the same one and you *are* thinking of indulging, do please wear a condom, Mummy – that is to say, get him to wear one rather, because things have changed since your day, and that brief moment of pleasure now can bring death and destruction later. But don't let me put you off.

I'm going to have to sign off now, reluctantly, as it's my turn to comb the sheep. Honestly, you wouldn't believe how untidy they get – a farmer's work is never done!

Dearest sweetest darlingest Moo Ma (do you remember I used to call you that as a little boy? Aaaaah!), I've read and re-read all your letters over the last few weeks, and I simply cannot understand why you're being so intransigent. Is it just that you've become so institutionalised that you are afraid of life beyond your prison walls? If it is, we could help you through that. You could stay in your room for the first week – we could even *lock* you in if it made you feel more at home. Please think about it. And don't give up on the I Ching, – it changed my life back in '72, and I can never thank it enough.

Write soon. Or even better, come out soon.

All my love,
Your little
Howie
xxx
xx
x
!

THE TRAGIC STORY OF VERA SMALL

by *Shagthorne Gazette* Reporter

NIGEL NORRIS

LOCAL HERO Les Spatchcock (pictured above having a light-hearted moment with a French stick and an apple, 'Potting the Green') entertained a small but select crowd last Saturday at the 'Vera Small Is Mad Appeal' Fork and Finger Buffet.

Vera, mother of Howard Small of Sheepdipper's Shed – renowned throughout the length and breadth of Shale for his delicious organic sheep's yoghurt, available at attractive wholesale prices for bulk orders – claims that she was wrongly accused of being a drugs baron who preyed on the weak-willed and disillusioned in her native Little Potterton, and is currently awaiting trial on the high-security prison ship, HMS *Pride of Cleveland*, at anchor off the east coast.

While Vera languishes in her cell, her family and friends are working tirelessly for her release. A regular churchgoer (I counted at least two dog-collars among the enthusiastic supporters) and a pensioner who served her country on the home front during the last war, Vera was a pillar of her local community, organising Bring and Buys, spearheading the campaign for compulsory poop-and-scoop for pet-owners on her village green and being an inspiration to the Friends of St Peter's flower arranging circle. Now, typically, she is refusing to appeal for bail or even to consider her defence, because she feels her work 'inside' among the prisoners is more important than her own personal survival. Anybody who watches *Prisoner: Cell Block H* can imagine the appalling conditions under which she must be working, but nevertheless Vera Small is adamant that she will stay and do her duty, and try to succeed where government educational reforms have failed. So far her perseverance has succeeded – rumour has it that every prisoner on board HMS *Pride of Cleveland* can now write her own name.

(continued on page 2)

128

(continued from front page)

BUT VERA ISN'T STOPPING THERE

Speaking on her behalf, the prison chaplain, Reverend Trevor Bull, said, 'Vera won't rest until all her pupils can fill out a DHSS claim form without her help, and without copying from their neighbour. The prisoners are rising gallantly to the challenge, and when I last saw them two days ago were busy sucking their pencils over "previous employment".'

If you would like to help the Vera Small Is Mad Appeal, please send contributions c/o the *Gazette*. And if you're interested in the Vera Small Prisoners' Literacy Campaign and have any old books you no longer need, please send them direct to Vera Small, HMS *Pride of Cleveland*, The Wash.

(Now turn to page 23 to see Les Spatchcock in more serious mode at Clangham Leisure Centre Professional Snooker Exhibition.)

26 May

My dear Howard (it really is time you gave up your baby
name – remember, you *are* nearly forty)

I'm very sorry about the hair. But I really don't see how
I can be to blame. Arnon has taught me many things (I
won't go into details just now, this letter may be censored)
but the most important by far is to rush towards guilt less
willingly. This is awkward for a person ready to admit to
everything from the burning of a saucepan to the
extermination of the Jews, but I find it easier in here where
none of you can get at me. Frankly, dear, what you choose
to do with your life is not my responsibility. Both of you
children have unique gifts – if you count Karen's ability to
shatter glass with her screams and cry long enough to
qualify for the *Guinness Book of Records* – now, to quote
Arnon's phrase, 'Just get off your butts and use them!'
I wish I could describe to you the liberation I have felt
in this prison cell. No mirrors to remind one of wrinkles
and warts; no telephone to interrupt at an inconvenient
moment; no dependants demanding love and protection;
above all no friends, with their expectations of your
behaviour and disappointment in it. Rest assured that
wherever Irene is she will be in charge. If she is indeed
'underground', she will be bossing around the seven
dwarfs and teaching the nastier of the trolls they'd better
mind their manners. Don't worry about her. She is a
survivor. I must say, the prospect of seeing any of you
again fills me with horror. Nor does the notion of living at
Sheepshedder's or whatever it's called enthral me. Hessian
is all very well in its place, which is not, in my opinion, on
the walls. Wool next to my skin makes me itch, so there's
no way I'm sleeping with a sheep on the bed. Then there's
the toilet facilities – all that health food and only one loo! I
make do with a slop bucket here, but at least it is mine

exclusively. No, no, Howie, it wouldn't work. Of course, if you were to consider the possibility of refurbishing the large front room with manmade fibres and an en-suite lavatory . . .

Must rush now. It's play-reading class. We're on the second act of *Les Miserables*, which has struck a chord with many of the inmates.

Some of my love,

Vera

PS The mystery ingredient was your father's hair tonic. I'm trying to remember what it was called so that you can try some.

The Gables
Little Potterton

14 July

Dear Vera,

I don't suppose you'll be interested, since you have apparently given up all concern for your erstwhile life 'outside', but I have moved into your old house for a while, and thank heavens I did! Some young people had 'squatted' in it (in more ways than one) and were charging admission to Acid House parties. Of course word has got round locally about your trouble with the police, and the teenagers think you're marvellous for being an OAP drugs baron. The tickets said 'Get off your face at Vera's place', whatever that means. Anyway, I chased them out and have put the house to rights as much as I can, although I'm afraid your crystal has gone the way of all things, and your Aunty Gertie's Victorian commode has had to be sent away to be destroyed.

I came here to get some peace away from Sheepdipper's Shed, and to indulge in some quiet reflection. In that respect I do miss prison life – being 'banged up' in solitary can sometimes be a blessing. I sold my house when I came out in order to pay our legal fees to the lady barrister and to fund your appeal. There's still some money left, so don't worry, I shan't be a drain on your resources, although I shall have to be careful if it is to last me my days.

I'm sorry you've decided to give up your fight and spend the rest of your allotted 'inside'. I had hoped that you and I would spend a jolly retirement together, perhaps travelling the world and doing everything that women of our generation could never do when our husbands were alive. Still, 'to each one his role' (Thought for the Day in today's *Daily Mirror*), and who am I to keep you from your destiny?

There's a lot of work still to be done here, but I'm tackling it little by little. The mint's done very well – it's taken over the entire garden – so I shall soon be bottling that like mad, as a sauce, to sell at the forthcoming Church Fête. Quite like old times, in a way, but somehow strangely different. The local community have welcomed me with open arms, and I have been invited to take over your position as Chairperson of the Little Potterton Poop-and-Scoop Campaign, which I have willingly undertaken. Of course, being a dog-owner lends a great deal of weight to the argument, and Sidney and I are busy setting a good example on the Village Green. There's also talk afoot of a new bypass scheme which, if built, would come straight through your patio, thereby making your picture window more like a Space Invaders screen. While there is breath left in me I shall fight it, but let's hope it doesn't come to that – with my track record with bulldozers, we know where *that* would end!

I am enclosing a few pressed sprigs of lavender, mint and thyme to remind you of an English country garden – I hope they still smell by the time they reach you.

I had a postcard from Lesley the other day. Keith has left her for another woman, and she's wondering if I'd like to go out there to look after Cheryl Marie while she gets on with her new career in real estate. I was half-tempted for a second, but on reflection decided against. Once you've got used to the idea that you're dispensable, it's not an unattractive existence by any means. And after my recent experiences with Karen and Sabrina I intend to give a wide berth to spoilt children in future.

All for now as the Vicar's coming round in a minute in his capacity as Treasurer of the Poop-and-Scoop to discuss the inevitable fund-raising. Does it never end?! Glad to hear that you're well and happy and are at last feeling fulfilled,

Kindest regards,

Irene

Sheepdipper's Shed

22 July

Dear Irene,

Snatching a few moments from washing nappies to put
pen to paper. Or rather, quill to recycled papyrus – excuse
the bumps and blotches. Can't say I'm entirely happy with
the nappies, which have turned an unpleasant magenta . . .
is it the ecology-conscious washing powder, or has Karen
been feeding beetroot to Sabrina? Frankly, nothing about
this place would surprise me. I have just cooked supper
for six adults (if you include Karen), a baby, twelve sheep,
three dogs, eleven cats, two goats and a donkey. Even
Jesus would have had trouble making a wholewheat loaf
and a couple of free-range trout go round that lot.

They are so incompetent, I can quite see why you left.
Normally I enjoy restoring order to chaos, but this has got
me stumped. Today, Howard gave two sacks of butter
beans and a Celtic Craft poncho to a girl collecting for
earthquake victims and Antony put a nail through a pipe
while trying to build a sauna. Karen keeps to her room all
day, thank heavens. She says she is 'proof-reading' but I
heard the distinct sound of snoring this afternoon. Hardly
surprising, as her nocturnal ramblings are becoming quite
legendary. She visits every pub in the village, then paddles
in the pond singing rude songs or abseils from the belfry. I
have most of the care of Sabrina. Fortunately, she is a little
love, and a charming shade of coffee.

Apart from that, things go on as normal. Howard's been
fitted for an NHS wig. We were very supportive, but
Karen had to ruin it all by suggesting he could play
Widow Twankey. We have a visiting Swami who meditates
on the lawn and dyed my new underwear orange, and an
out-of-work actor chum of Howard's who is 'helping' in

the shop. Clearly he has been helping himself, since the till has been out three days running.

I've just realised you must be wondering what on earth I am doing here. The last time we communicated I was still 'inside'. Well . . . whoops, there's been a terrible bang upstairs. Either Karen has fallen out of bed or Antony's blown up the central heating. Explanations soon, the availability of papyrus permitting.

In haste,

Vera

PS Everyone's pleased to know you're alive and well, in their own way. Howard murmured, 'She was such a dear,' and Karen said, 'Who's Irene?'

PPS What on earth do you mean, 'The mint has taken over'? I was *ruthless* with that patch for years. As soon as my back's turned, it runs amok. All I can say is, *be brutal!*

The Gables

28 July

My dear Vera,

Congratulations and felicitations! I can't get over the fact that you're back with us again – and in more ways than one, by the tone of your letter. I don't know which is more miraculous – your freedom or your friendliness. Thank goodness you're 'back to normal'. I tried to ring you, but I note that the Sheepdipper's phone has been cut off again. Howard is a hopeless businessman, I'm afraid to say. Last time he couldn't pay the bill because of cash-flow problems, he tried to barter with British Telecom with yoghurt. Imagine the administrative nightmares they would have had trying to distribute that to the shareholders!

Please do write post-haste and tell me all about it. Better still, come over and see me *soon*. Do you want your house back, or are you going to stay with the children for a while? I can easily move out as soon as you say the word. Audrey Roscoe (I've re-established contact with her recently, and I'm pleased to say she's much pleasanter these days) keeps on at me to go and stay with her again, so I could go there. (I must tell you in full one day the laughs we had about Clive once we'd broken the ice between us – it seems as if his old 'problem' reared its head with her as well – or rather, didn't rear its head, if you get my meaning.) But I digress. Let me know what you want as soon as you know yourself. Sidney's barking – I've told him your good news and that I'm writing to you at the moment, so I imagine he's sending his 'best regards'!

I'm intrigued to know how your release came about, and am wondering if it was anything to do with my protest? I've been writing non-stop to the Home Secretary, and after getting nowhere for weeks, I told him that if he didn't let you out straight away, I would pull out my teeth one by one and send them to him daily. This I have been doing for the last fortnight, and was beginning to despair of a result being obtained before the full set gave out. Don't worry, your 'friend' is neither toothless nor gaga. I've been cracking them out of Clive's old dentures with a pair of pliers. I hung on to them at first through sentimentality, but I knew they'd come in useful one day.

The other thing I've been up to is trying to focus some psychic powers on to you (Bruce, of course, is up in arms about it – I sometimes don't know why the Christian Church is so paranoid and small-minded if they know they're in the right). I've spent a fortune on mystical literature and artefacts, and have read the Tarot, the Runes, the tea-leaves and your hand (you'd left a nasty imprint on your mahogany wardrobe, which I've polished off now). And now you say that Karen's been doing it by reading the Proofs. What are they? I haven't come across them in my researches. You see, nobody is all bad. I'm sorry she's back drinking again, though. Antony gave her some special herbs to smoke instead, and they seemed to do the trick for a while, but I believe they are hard to come by and rather expensive. Really, you'd think that if the Department of Health was genuinely anxious about alcoholism they'd give these things out on prescription, wouldn't you? I had a tiny go on them myself, and thoroughly enjoyed it, even though I'm not a smoker personally.

Anyway, all for now as I'm anxious not to miss the post, and Sidney is showing signs of wanting to set a shining example of poop-and-scoop hygiene on the village green. I am enclosing some sheets of your own personalised stationery so you can dispense with the papyrus. Honestly, the things we've written on lately! It's worse than the war with 'make do and mend'. It was lovely to hear from you –

such a welcome surprise – and I can't wait to see your old smiling face again. I shan't put 'with love', since it caused such a rumpus between us last time, but believe me, I do send you

My kindest, sincerest regards,

Irene

The Bluebell B & B
Lower Shagthorne
Derbs.

5 August

My dear Irene,

At last I've had time to digest your letters properly. Talking of digest, I'm relieved about the teeth. One turned up in the *Cleveland*'s Sunday gruel but I assumed it was the cook's – he and the *sous-chef* had violent relations. As you'll see, I've moved into a B & B in the village. Sheepdipper's was getting me down, what with the cooking and chanting and living life as a constant 'celebration'. And don't talk to *me* about runes; Antony's up to his elbows in them!

Well, you'll be hopping with curiosity about my release. It was all Arnon's doing. He explained to me that staying 'inside' was 'fulfilling my need to be needed' and that now my literacy class had mastered *Janet and John* I could leave them to themselves with the reading. I must say, keeping up was becoming an effort. I mean, I love a good read but Nietzsche *is* rather trying, especially without reading glasses. Once I'd decided to make my bid for freedom, Arnon took over. He said he'd give me some LSD (no, not money, that's the mistake *I* made) and that we'd leave the rest to fortune. It was very dramatic. Apparently I shredded a sail with my bare hands and splintered the deck with a hatchet, then I shinned up the topmast, stripped and sang 'Jerusalem' and offered oral sex to the bo'sun. All I can remember is seeing stars, but that was probably when they knocked me out, as I came to in a strait-jacket. It was the talk of the ship for days; there was no end of pipe-tapping. Eventually the governor signed a release form, putting me in care of the community. It seems that if you are mad you are safer on the outside;

everyone there is doolally. Howard and Antony came to fetch me and I saw my last glimpse of HMS *Cleveland* from the back of their van – they'd thoughtfully cut a couple of holes in the lentil sack I was tied in.

It took me a while to recover. I kept getting 'flashes' (rather like flushes, but brighter) but on my second day Karen accused me of being lazy, so that got me up and doing. From then till now I haven't sat down, except cross-legged to do Yoga, and I am completely exhausted.

About the house – stay as long as you like, though I must say, I do miss the garden. The shale at Shag is very unrewarding. I often sat at my prison window gazing through the bars at the restless waves and daydreaming of Little Potterton's loamy pastures. Of course my lawn was only twelve by eight, but its verdant green was delightful. How true those sentiments (Wordsworth's, I think) about being closer to God in a garden. Not, I'm afraid, that I believe in God. There, I've said it. I'm sorry if it offends. I know you've always been in close contact with the Divine (or at least, with His earthly representatives) but I've come to the conclusion that it's a gigantic con trick to keep women in their place. Ask yourself who it is who arranges the flowers, irons the vestments, scrubs the flags, bakes the cakes and, yes, who sits in those uncomfortable pews while some ridiculous twit drones on about duty and self-sacrifice? I confided my doubts to Rev. Trev (remember him?) in the days after my shipboard frenzy. He said I should use them in my testimony as further proof of madness.

Your offer of a touring retirement in parts unknown is certainly very attractive, but what, I wonder, would we fund it with? Karen is trying to take over what remains of my meagre resources (I've been paying the mortgage on Sheepdipper's since before I went 'inside') on the grounds that I'm officially insane, but so far I've resisted. Perhaps we should write a book about our exploits!

I'm so very tired I must lie down. Write soon with a few of your cheery words.

Your ever dear friend,

Vera

PS I can't recommend Audrey for an indefinite stay. She's a good soul, but she hasn't much of a sense of humour.

PPS Of course, I am indispensable at Sheepdipper's. I run up there every day. Sabrina is teething and needs constant attention. When I pointed that out to Karen, she snarled that it was more than *she*'d got!

The Gables

10 August

Dear Vera,

Thank you for your letter. What an extraordinary story regarding your release! In fact, what an extraordinary turn our lives have taken altogether! It's almost as if we'd never lived before, what with the mundane round of bottling and jamming and Bring and Buys. And now we've both been in prison, both survived it stronger and wiser and with, I think, a stronger sense of life's adventure. The things we've seen and done! The words we've learned! What *is* oral sex? You didn't bite him in the privates, did you?!

Be all that as it may, I can't help feeling rather depressed. We've lost so much. I've lost my home and you may lose yours. Another meeting of the Beat the Bypass group last night revealed that they are 99 per cent sure that they are going ahead, and will be compensating owners to a ridiculously low level, based on the poor current house prices. After all our pressure, the only change they've made to their plans is to shift it over a few feet so that it will now come straight through your lounge instead of running outside it. I mean, what kind of a bypass is that?! I don't think the group is going to fight it any more. To be honest, they've got everything to gain by not doing. Yours and Mabel Thrush's old houses are the only ones to be affected, and the rest of them will enjoy the benefits of no longer having juggernauts getting stuck on the bend at the Jolly Jackdaw. The new people at Mabel's were going to leave anyway due to a posting abroad (lucky them), and they're pretty relieved, what with the property market, that they'll get any money at all.

So what to do? Where to go to live out our days? And what on? Now that I know you're safe and well, I've been concentrating my psychic powers on drawing good luck and money to us both. I don't know if it's had any effect your end, but so far nothing has happened here. I tend to agree with you about God and the Church – it is all a con trick to keep us in our place. But I feel very strongly that there must be something else, some reason for living, some rhythm to life, some force of good (and equally of evil), some Otherness or Isness linking us all to the whole, or *some*thing. Damn it – someone at the door, just when I'd got into my flow. Hang on.

Well! I don't know what to say! You'll never guess what's happened now. My dear – my prayers are answered! I can't believe it can be true! You remember the demo at Grossthorpe links which led to my arrest – how could you forget! As always, we desperately needed funds at the time, so Arthur Snushall organised a raffle, and I showed willing by buying two books. After all this time, the blithering thing has been drawn, and I've won – First Prize! And you'll never guess what it is – a Dormobile camping van, fully fitted and equipped, donated by Ted and Marie Bellman after they splashed out on their Winnebago. It's a *home*, Vera, on *wheels*! What adventures we could have! Are you game? DO say yes! Let's take off and see the world – I've always wanted to, but never got past Marbella.

Vera, this proves my point – there is a purpose to prayer and positive thinking, and magic *does* exist. Even my tea-leaves indicated something of this nature this morning, but I was too down in the mouth to take any notice. Vera, I dare you to come with me and see the world! What have we got to lose? Write back sooner than soon, and heigh-ho, Silver, away!

Your buccaneering friend,

Irene

PS And what would Arnon say about your PPS? Break the mould! Be irresponsible and dispensable before you die!

The Bluebell B & B

14 August

My dear Irene,

My first response to your letter was a whoop of joy. Only the Bluebell's pet parrot responded, the rest of the residents being too deaf, or perhaps dead, to notice. How wonderful to have nothing, except for Ted and Marie's Dormobile of course, and how timely your news. Yesterday I heard that my bank manager has made some terrible errors with standing orders (victim of an illness known as 'Business Lunch Syndrome'). As a result I have defaulted on all mortgage and life insurance payments and the building society are about to repossess. Let them. See how they enjoy living in the fast lane. Literally. I'll cash in what's left of the life insurance – I was only hanging on to it to pay for my funeral – and Up, Up and Away! I can't wait to be tucked up in those dear little bunk beds. I'm so over the moon (would the moon be going *too* far, d'you think?) I'm going to make myself a cup of hotel-bedroom instant coffee to celebrate!

Later
There's only one thing. I won't be doing all the driving. Now you've passed your test there's no excuse, and I can't abide a back-seat driver. I'll never forget you punching me in the ear as you 'instructed' me with hand gestures to 'go round the bend' on the Horseshoe Pass. We were lucky to escape with minor injuries. No. Irene, it's in the front and behind the wheel, or we'll be going nowhere.

Later
By the by, how big is this Dormobile? Space is so important in relationships, Arnon taught me that. I mean,

I wouldn't call you *territorial*, exactly, but you did put all my things in the corner when I stayed and cover them with a dustsheet. You were also particular on soiled undies, I recall. You gave me a plastic carrier bag so they wouldn't sully the bedroom. Then there are other . . . more 'personal' . . . functions. A home on wheels is just the place to discover the worst about toilet-training. As for possessive! I thought you were going to call the police the day I went out with your brolly. How will you be with the foreign food? You can't abide a Coquille St Jacques and the natives are devils for garlic. Come to that, how will you be with the natives? Oh dear, oh dear, I *am* sounding churlish and after your lovely letter . . . But I can't help feeling that we've had our ups and downs and that was when we were living apart. How will we be *together*?

Still later

Rushed up to Sheepdipper's with a matinée jacket I've been crocheting in the evenings. They were all in a terrible state about the money. Howard was weeping into a soya bean casserole and Karen had hit the vodka bottle. She wasn't a bit grateful for the jacket and said what was I trying to do, make ethnic history by getting Sabrina to win the Miss Pears competition? I didn't say anything. Later, when she told me it was time for Sabrina's bath I pointed out that it was her turn, Sabrina was *her* baby. She gave me a very peculiar look and snapped she was glad I'd remembered. I think Antony was sorry for me. He gave me a set of runes so I'm throwing them madly.

Next morning

The runes said journey so I've settled my bill. Popped into the library for some Linguaphone records – I know you're a stickler for pronunciation. I got French, Italian, German, Spanish, Cameroons, Hindu and Swahili. NB

Must remember to get an international driving licence. You too.

Later

Last visit to Sheepdipper's to say goodbye. Howard's very excited. He's found a financial backer – some local chap who'd been dabbling in stripped pine, then his partner went off with another chap and now he wants something substantial. The soya bean casserole should be just the ticket. Showed Karen how to care for the seeds I've sown and tended. I'm wasting my time, they'll be dead in a week. She doesn't know a radish from a nettle. I'm popping down to Buxton for a couple of days to buy some suitable clothing – there's nothing more adventurous than a duvet coat in Shagthorne.

> The Bull & Pestle
> Dyke Lane
> Buxton

I've spent up. A lurex sarong, striped beach outfit, emerald taffeta ballgown, cerise cocktail number, two dozen espadrilles and a gorgeous two-piece bathing suit for you in primrose and vermilion. Drop me a note at the above. All being well, I leave Friday.

Next morning

Woke in tears with a terrible sense of loss. Oh, Irene, we will be all right, won't we?

The Gables

19 August

Dear Vera,

My first response to *your* letter was, 'All right then, forget it.' Talk about looking a gift horse in the mouth and recommending orthodontistry! Talk about ungrateful, ungracious and just plain bloody rude! Talk about limiting somebody's growth potential by reminding them that they are the nastiest, most unreasonable person you know, and implying that any change for the better is impossible. Really, it sometimes seems to me that you regard yourself as the perfect centre of a disappointingly imperfect universe. Haven't you learned *anything* at *all* through all your psychotherapy? Or does it only apply to you? Oh yes, it's all very well for *you* to carp and cavil – we're all in the wrong, you're the only one in the right. Have you ever stopped to wonder why both your children turned out to be total incompetents?

But my second response was, 'Rise above it, Irene, she's probably over-tired.' Certainly, I can think of no other reason that you'd spend all your petrol money on ball gowns and lurex sarongs. And why buy me a bikini? Do you think I can't look after my *own* beachwear? Personally I am travelling light, and I can tell you now that the Dormobile is *small* so unless your emerald taffeta folds down to the size of a pacamac, forget it.

My third response – and you'll see I'm getting it more in perspective and feeling less angry all the time – is that it is only right and proper for you to express your fears, as it is only right and proper for me to express mine. Yes, you've hit the nail on the head, change is very frightening. But what's the alternative? What use has fear been to us all our lives? It kept me unhappily married to a man who despised me, who told me I was a fool, and who couldn't keep his hands off our dinner guests. I'm damned if I'm going to make the same mistake twice, particularly at this late stage in my journey through life. 'Onwards, ever onwards' is *my* battle-cry for the rest of my allotted, but don't let me stop you from staying rooted in the mire of your own misery until death do you part, I'm sure.

My fourth response – and now I'm getting calmer and more constructive all the time, as I think you'll agree – is to reassure you that we'll work it out if we both keep our senses of humour and try to live and let live. If, for instance, it proves to be that I can't stand being cooped up in a confined space with your dreadful, earth-shattering snoring, I shall try to maintain the attitude that you're not doing it for the sole purpose of driving me round the bend, to borrow your phrase. And talking of which, I intend to do *most* of the driving, thank you very much, particularly as it seems that I shall be buying the petrol.

But just in case we temporarily lose our senses of humour and our easygoing attitudes, perhaps we should make a rule. Like counting to ten before we speak again. Or saying 'Sollocks' like Amanda and Elyot in *Private Lives*. (I played Amanda to Cyril Organ's Elyot in 1958, and even Clive had to admit that my performance was hysterical.) Or, and perhaps this might be best of all and most apposite for us, maybe we should communicate only in writing if we're having a set-to, thereby giving a chance for tempers to cool and reason to take over. Think about it. The world is very large, as Elyot told Amanda, and it's going to take us a very long time to get round it, Vera, so we're going to have to pack a great deal of patience and humour. But then, what else has a life with Clive fitted me for, I ask myself?

So, if you feel up to the challenge, I shall pick you up at the Bull & Pestle at 10.00 a.m. on Friday, and we'll motor straight down to Dover, cross on the ferry and be in France by the time the sun is over the yardarm. Here's to it! The next time we communicate in writing will be because one *or other* of us is being selfish and unreasonable, I imagine, so I'll take this opportunity of reminding you (in writing, so you don't forget) that I am very fond of you, despite all your foibles, and I wish you only happiness, contentment and great adventures!

Sincerest and heartfelt regards,

Irene x

(An autoroute outside Calais)

Irene!

When I screamed 'Right! Right!' I was not agreeing that the driver of the approaching truck was a 'blitherin' Froggie cretin'. I, like him, was in fear for my life. They drive on the right in this country!

PS I counted to ten before I wrote this, but at this rate it needs to be forty.

V.

More Ladies of Letters

Foreword

Marbella University

Ten years ago my friends, Carole Hayman and Lou Wakefield, were kind enough to send me a batch of letters they had found in the drawer of a melamine cabinet at a boot fair in Kent.

These letters were part of a correspondence between a Mrs Irene Spencer and a Mrs Vera Small, women in their early sixties, and recorded the beginning of their friendship.

At that time my collection of historical documents was relatively small and had not yet become the all-embracing passion of my life. However, I recognised that the Spencer/Small Letters, (as they have since become known), were potentially, extremely valuable, both in literary and financial terms. Few collectors at the time were interested in English domestic correspondence; especially that written by older women. Now, of course, with the widespread use of electronic communication devices, letters of any type have become extremely rare. When not on loan to University libraries and museums my Spencer/Small letters are kept in a vault at Coutts, together with other rare collectable documents.

Imagine my delight and surprise last year when a courier interrupted my study of a Sir Cliff Richard letter (to a fisherman pal on the Algarve) and handed me a large jiffy bag which bulged with yet more Spencer/Small letters! I was suspicious at first; there are many forgeries on the market. A period of rigorous investigation followed. I am particularly grateful to Professor Okawa of Nagasaki University for his invaluable work on 'the use of the ironic single quote in the letters of Vera Small'. This work helped to verify the letters. As did the work of Dr Karen Pigg of De Montfort University, who's dissertation, 'the later poetry of Irene Spencer – the voice of exile' provided me with yet more evidence that this latest batch of letters was indeed genuine. I will be forever grateful to the anonymous person who sent me these letters.

Because I was frantically busy with my new book, 'Ted Hughes – collected notes to the milkman' I asked Ms Wakefield and Ms Hayman to edit these latest Small/Spencer letters. They proved to be extremely sensitive editors. All libellous and unnecessarily cruel statements made by Irene and Vera about myself and my so called 'exploitation of private papers' have been removed, as have frequent libellous references to senior members of the Royal Family.

More Ladies of Letters provides us with an invaluable insight into the mindset of the contemporary British pensioner. The book raises many questions: did the feminist movement (see footnote 1)[1] concentrate too much on the bra and neglect the support hose? Has Irene and Vera's heavy use of saturated fats over the years contributed to the dysfunctionalisation of their respective families? The renowned sexologist, Dr Marcus Cox, wrote in *Sexology Today* (Jan 5 1999), 'After reading the Spencer/Small letters I had to re-evaluate my life's work regarding the sexual appetite of the older woman.'

More Ladies of Letters is, however, very accessible and will appeal to the common reader. It is not only an historical document, it is a fascinating glimpse into the private worlds of two extraordinarily ordinary English women.

Sue Townsend
2000

---

[1] The advocacy of women's rights on the ground of the equality of the sexes

Dear Vera,

DO NOT TEAR THIS UP. Read it first and then decide.

You will no doubt be surprised that I am writing to you after we both vowed never to communicate with each other again after the disastrous 'holiday' together last year. However a certain event has taken place which I feel duty bound to inform you of. I have tussled with my conscience as to whether to keep my distance and keep mum, but I find I cannot lie, not even (as politicians seem to do) by emission.

There is no nice way to impart the dreadful news I have to tell you. Bill Snapes is dead. You remember, of course, after dallying with us both, he set up with a girl half his age, and I think I told you they'd had a baby. I seem to recall us enjoying the joke of him having to change nappies again in his late sixties (she was a career girl, and as he was retired he became the 'house-husband'). Well, no sooner did she have that baby but another one popped out, and the upshot is that he had a heart attack last week from which he hasn't recovered, and the funeral is on Friday. The village is buzzing with the rumour that he was taking Niagra, which just goes to show what happens if you try to burn the candle at both ends. Certainly, since it happened, the queue at the chemist's has gone down considerably, and his old golf-ing cronies are looking far less jaunty.

I know that you were once 'fond' of him, so in the circumstances, if you do want to pay your respects at the service, which is at three in the afternoon, you could stay overnight with me on the put-you-up in the living room. I have already checked the buses and trains and found that there is no way you could get back afterwards, unless you spend the night on the platform at Nottingham, where you'd have to change.

Incidentally, since I'm writing anyway, I thought I'd just mention that I found your swimming costume the other week rolled up inside my old pacamac which I was about to donate to the Village Minellium Bus Shelter fund. I told you there would be a perfectly good explanation for its disappearance, which did not involve me stealing it either to wear myself or to make you less attractive on the beach next to me. I won't enclose it now as it would be a waste of postage stamps if you're coming over next week, and anyway, as you'll see for yourself, the elastic has gone in the legs. When I think of all the trouble it caused! But far be it from me to point the finger of blame, or to rake up ancient history, and anyway, the red wine came out of my cream skirt on the third wash, so as far as *I'm* concerned, the hatchet is well and truly buried.

Can you let me know of your intentions either way as soon as possible so I can give young Tracey Snapes an idea of numbers?

Best wishes,

Irene Spencer

Sheepdipper's Shed
Shooters Hill
Shale, Shap,
Nr Great Shagthorne
Derbs.

Wed.

Dear Irene,

I was covered in shame on receipt of your letter. (I was
also covered in sheep's yoghurt – your opening phrase
was so alarming, I thought it was one of those dreadful
chain letters which plague the vulnerable, and I dropped
the hand-thrown pot all over me.) Shame, because it's
been on my mind to write to you for months, particularly
after I found several photos of us on that very holiday
when I was clearing my room at the nursing home.
Remember that lovely Italian man who insisted on snap-
ping us at the Trevi fountain? You had just called me a
blithering idiot for tossing in the equivalent of five
pounds in lire. Foreign coins are so confusing. He caught
what I like to think is the essential you, grimacing, with
your handbag raised as though you were about to strike
me. I did have a laugh, and it put me in mind of so many
similar occasions over the years we have known each
other.

As you see, I am at Howard's. I came here after a
brief sojourn at 'Golden Pastures' residential home. I'd
had a nasty bout of flu which led to slight deafness,
but Karen decided my blank stare when she was
screaming something about her latest love tangle was

161

incipient Alzheimer's and persuaded Howard to
commit me to long-term care for the elderly. Lord save
us from over-dramatic daughters! I got my hearing
back and left after a fortnight, though I must say I was
tempted to stay longer – it was very pleasant to have
all one's meals prepared, even though the cocoa did
taste funny. I am now waiting for sheltered accommodation to become vacant. I suppose that means waiting
for one of the poor old dears to die, talking of funerals.
I never thought I would wish it on anybody, but life at
Sheepdipper's Shed, even with one's favourite child, is
a little trying. The sheep's yoghurt has not been doing
at all well since all that fuss about BSC affecting dairy
products and some days I'm at my wits' end as to how
to use up sixty gallons. Perhaps I should take a leaf
out of Cleopatra's book and bath in it! Might be preferable to tepid, solar-heated water with the pungent
aroma of night soil – the toilet facilities here have not
improved, despite Howard and his partner, Antony,
having created their own personal cesspit.

Poor Bill. A case of what goes around, comes around.
Or what goes up must come down, if he really was
taking Niagra. Oh, my goodness, I've just realised
Friday is the day after tomorrow, they've taken so long
to forward your letter. The matron at Golden Pastures
is a little disorganised. I once surprised her with a
bottle of sherry poised over a mug, at nine-thirty in the
morning.

Of course I'll come. It's only proper. Besides, I'm
curious for a glance at this Tracey. I'd love to stay, if
only for the hot water. I'll taxi to yours from the
station and change. Oh dear, what on earth will I

wear? Howard went through my wardrobe when I arrived and chucked out everything in man-made fibres. That reminds me, by all means give that bathing costume to the Bus Shelter fund. Perhaps someone with large thighs will buy it. Howard is planning the 'Biggest Party the Derby Dales Has Known' for New Year's Eve '99. He's asked me to help with the catering. At last a use for the yoghurt! I despair at having to think up more recipes, but anything I can do to help the Millennium . . .

Will jump on Howard's bike and pedal this the four miles to the post. (Really, you can take this eco stuff too far. Howard and Antony *do* live up a 1 in 4 hill.) Look forward to seeing you, if I survive it.

All the best,

Vera

The Limes
Saturday

Dear Howard,

It is with great regret that I write to tell you that
your mother has had an accident while staying here
with me, but is not seriously ill. I have not yet ascertained the exact details of the full circumstances of her
fall, as her dentures broke during the incident and her
lips have swollen up like balloons, so she's making
even less sense than usual. Suffice it to say that, as
usual, the combination of strong drink and a member
of the opposite sex had a disastrous effect on her. And
not only on her. The 'gentleman' in question fortunately escaped with a black eye and a broken toe, but
Tracey Snapes's pelargoniums will never be the same
again. And all of this during the baked meats of
Tracey's husband's funeral! I was so embarrassed I
didn't know where to put myself. But then again, what
did I expect? Your Mother has never given me anything
but trouble.

The hospital released her because they didn't have a
bed, so now neither have I and am forced to make use of
my put-you-up in the living room, which with my back
is like sleeping on a time bomb. Is there any way you can
arrange to take her back to Sheepdipper's Shed to finish
her convalescence with you? Quite frankly I'm
exhausted, and she's only been here a day and a half.
Besides, I'm sure the country air would do her more
good than being cooped up here in my bedroom.

Unfortunately there has been a misunderstanding
with the cable company and I am currently without a

phone, so please write back immediately and let me know what you intend to do. And whatever it is, make it quick.

Hope you're well by the way, and kind regards to Antony.

With all good wishes,

Irene

The Limes
Saturday

Dear Howard,

I don't know what Irene has told you and I don't want
to call her a liar, but it definitely isn't true. There *was* a
small incident, I'll admit, but nothing like on the scale
she has been suggesting and certainly not for the reasons!

The funeral was a pleasant enough affair. Can't say I
took much to Tracey Snapes, she's gone past her bloom
very quickly. I'm sure living with Bill and two small children was no picnic, or perhaps it was too many! She's
put on so much weight and with her bottle blonde hair,
she reminded me of a chat show hostess. She'd omitted to
follow Bill's last instructions (no doubt getting even when
he can't answer back) and the wake was an alcohol-free
zone. One of Bill's golfing compadres, Barry Rowbotham
and I were chatting in the conservatory . . . Barry's a
smoker, though only cigars. Needless to say, Tracey didn't
have the heating on and Barry, a charming man, was kind
enough to offer me a drop of warming whisky in my tea.
We soon got tripping down memory lane about Bill.
Barry was a hoot, showing me some of his tricks with a
golf club. (Unfortunately Tracey had left some pelargoniums . . . well, that's what she called them, they looked like
common or garden geraniums to me . . . rather too close
to the edge of a shelf and three or four did get broken.)

Barry is also a ballroom-dancing champ, he's got
international trophies. Unfortunately his partner is in
hospital at the moment with several slipped discs and
he was telling me how much he missed it. Well, you

know how familiar *I* am with the dance floor! In no time he was demonstrating a couple of tricky steps in the Paso Doble, which has always been one of my favourites. Some people might say, indeed they did, and Irene was one of them, that dancing at a funeral shows disrespect. I had to remind her of the many rituals we had seen on our travels where those in mourning were wearing considerably less than a lounge suit and a heliotrope two-piece. However . . .

The tiled floor in the conservatory was unusually slippery, possibly a film of ice due to the freezing temperature, and, executing a flamboyant bull charge, I skidded, stepped on Barry's toe, threw out an arm to save myself and punched him in the eye. Easily done, as I'm sure you'll agree. We both fell to the ground. Irene said afterwards we 'crashed' and 'rolled around on top of one another', but that's a wild exaggeration. I have tried to explain what really happened but my dentures have sustained irreparable damage, which makes speaking difficult and Irene swears she can't read my writing, which after all our years of correspondence is a bit rich. Staying with her, under the circumstances, is very trying and I'd be grateful if you could come and get me as soon as possible. It is awkward to manage the train in plaster.

Irene has just come in and brusquely informed me that it will take six weeks to replace my teeth on the NHS, so I must stop now and attempt to stick them together with some blue-tack. Oh, for a *Blue Peter* for the elderly!

Your loving Mumsie xx

PS Careful with that Niagra . . . Barry tells me it's easy to overdo it. Irene implied that's what we were testing on the conservatory floor.

Sheepdipper's Shed

Monday

Dear Irene

How lovely to hear from you after all this time, albeit in such painful circumstances. Mumsie's letter arrived by the second post, adding to the confusion. I think it's better to correspond directly with you, though, given the Alzheimer's situation. Poor Mumsie, she does have a way of courting disaster. Which limbs did she break exactly? Life on a mountain is tough enough, without milking sheep with both arms in plaster. Even worse if it's her legs. How will she manage a bicycle?

Still, needs must and we won't abandon her. We approached the hospital in Great Shagthorne about an ambulance, but the triage nurse (although he's a pet) said with all her problems she just didn't qualify as salvageable. His advice was a quick pillow over the face, but I'm sure he was only joking!

Antony is talking to our cheese man about borrowing his delivery van. We can lie her full length in that, which is more than we can in the MG Midget! All being well, we'll be with you the day after tomorrow.

Fondest regards, and a big kiss for Mumsie
(not on her swollen lips).

Howard

PS We long for something as adult as cable. Sadly, it hasn't reached the dull old Derby Dales.

Wednesday night

Dear Howard,

Wednesday has come and gone with neither sight nor sound of you. Did you mean you'd be arriving the day after tomorrow from you writing your note, or the day after tomorrow of me receiving it? Quite frankly I am being run ragged here with demands for this and demands for that, and what with your mother's teeth going west and everything having to be puréed, and my blender giving up the ghost and having to do it all by hand through a sieve, and then her having an accident on the bedsheets with the beetroot borscht, I really don't think I could be held responsible if something DREADFUL HAPPENED . . . My blood pressure has ROCKETED and the way I am feeling at the moment one or other of us may be in great danger of death.

I had to pause there. Water was coming through the living-room ceiling on to my head, as you'll notice from the runny ink. She'd fallen asleep in the bath with the tap running and her foot jammed in the overflow. Naturally she survived.

If you haven't arrived tomorrow to take her away I am afraid I will have to send her on to you in a mini-cab, COD.

Yours

Irene

Sunday 20th October

Dear Vera,

I hope your journey back to Sheepdipper's went all right in the van last month, and that you survived the smell of the Gorgonzola. And I hope that your leg is feeling better, and that the Bostick on your dentures dried eventually without sticking your gums together as feared. As you will see from the contents of this parcel, you left a couple of undergarments behind, laundered and enclosed. I'm also enc-ing some home made fudge that you should be able to manage to suck even if you still can't chew. I bought it from Mrs Appleyard, who is renowned for her confectionery, at the Home Fayre stall of the Minellium Bus Shelter Bring and Buy yesterday. A couple of people from the funeral were there – Ida Loseby and Mona Postlethwaite, I don't know if you remember them but they remember you – and they asked after you and told me to send you their best.

It's hard to find the words, but I'm hoping that in time the dust may settle on this recent visit of yours, and that we can put behind us our hasty words. I bumped into Barry Rowbotham last week in the super-market, and he was quick to take all the blame for the incident at the funeral. Thinking about it since – and you know what I'm like for dwelling on things until I've got them thoroughly sorted through – I've realised it was inevitable that we would get tense with each other at Bill's funeral, after all the trouble he caused between us so long ago. It was two years before we managed to speak again after I found you in bed together, if you remember, and – you may not know this, for you certainly didn't hear it from me – he had asked me only the day before if I'd consider taking the marital plunge. I really think that, all things being equal, if we could get over that, we can get over this.

In pensive mood I got out all your old letters today, and some rough copies of mine (I always like to neaten up mistakes afterwards, and usually make a fair copy of my missives) and I realised that the only time we have trouble between us is when we are actually together in the flesh. I was reminded how much I miss your cheery letters when we're at loggerheads and not speaking. I don't know what it is about you, but I just seem to find you more palatable in print.

Can bygones be bygone? Could we stick to the written word, do you think, and resist the temptation to meet? As you pointed out once in one of your notelets, there is a relief in being able to confide in someone outside the daily circle. I know for my part that it's nice to think that, after unburdening oneself, one's most sensitive secrets will not be touring the village before one can even get back home after being probed in the post office by wagging tongues and flapping ears. (Re-reading that, I find it to be what I think they call a mixed metaphor, but I am putting it in my fair copy because I can't think how it would be better, and I think you'll understand.)

Vera, it's hard to say it, but I'm sorry for my part if I caused offence during your stay. I was tetchy and under some strain. There. Now to the post box with this before I change my mind. Time will tell if you feel the same.

With fond regards and hopeful thoughts,

Your erstwhile friend

Irene

The Homely Faggot
Western Esplanade
Vicker-upon-St Agnes

Friday

Dear Irene,

Really, I've never known anyone like you for meeting trouble half-way. Except perhaps Audrey Roscoe. As you can see I am staying with her to recuperate. I'd had all I could take of Sheepdipper's. Howard would insist on plunging my leg in sheep's urine. Some ethnic health practice Antony picked up. Thank goodness they didn't extend it to the dentures.

Anyway, you will be pleased to know I am much better. In fact, as Karen said when I saw her last week and expressed surprise at her tattoo – apparently she's had it two years – 'Mother's back to normal.'

Speaking of memory loss, of course I remember Ida and Mona. Ida's the one whose husband was a transvestite and Mona's the one you said looked like a teletubby. But I don't recall what these 'words' were. You insisted you couldn't understand a thing I said, hasty or otherwise. Certainly *you* raised your voice more than was strictly necessary. But I put that down to your distress over Bill. I am more sensitive than you realise. I know perfectly well you've been carrying a candle for that two-timing creep for years and, in my opinion, it's a good thing he's dead. Especially living so close to you. Now you can move on with your life, Irene, instead of hoping he will ever come back.

You've missed a lot of chances. There was that nice Italian policeman on our trip, and the mechanic who mended the Dormobile . . .

Audrey's just come back in with the fish and news that there's sheltered accommodation going near the beach. I shall pop down tomorrow and investigate. All for now and rest assured your secrets are safe with me. And Audrey Roscoe.

Love, as always,

Vee

Saturday

Dear Irene,

Just had to send you a card with the good news. I got the accommodation! It's not exactly sheltered, unless you count the cliff, but it is near the beach. In fact it's on it. The last incumbent, poor soul, went out for a paddle and never came back. It's an ill wind . . . I am now the proud tenant of a caravan. It's in a large park with all mod cons and facilities . . . bet you can't wait to visit!

Vee

PS Write care of Audrey Roscoe

Lodge 202
Far Shores Trailer Park
Vicker-upon-St Agnes

Sunday

Dear Howard,

Thanks for forwarding Irene's letter. What happened
to the undies and home-made fudge? I can't think
either would be much use at Sheepdipper's, what with
your aversion to nylon and Antony's to sugar. Perhaps
you could send them now, so I can put Irene's mind at
rest. What an old misery guts she is!

Actually I shall need a few more of my possessions,
as you'll be glad to hear I have found a place to live. At
least temporarily. There is a transient feel to a 'mobile
home', though it's up to its axles in concrete. I want
cleaning equipment, wellington boots and the ghetto-
blaster. Perhaps you could store the rest in the barn, as
the space here is quite limited.

Your ever-loving Mumsie xx

Tuesday

Dear Vera,

Is there *anyone* in your acquaintance who is as perfect as you? In the first few lines of your letter you manage to insult me, your only begotten son, Howard, and his 'partner', and poor old Audrey Roscoe. Strange, since the one thing that we have in common is that we have all recently extended the hand of friendship to you and put you up – leave aside putting up with you.

I don't know *where* to start with your wild and inaccurate observations. I have not been 'carrying a candle' for Bill (or a torch, for that matter, which I believe is the usual nomenclature). As far as I'm concerned, it was over before it had begun, practically. It is true that I was once foolish enough to feel warmly towards him all those years ago when he first became my 'gentleman friend', but once you and he started to see each other behind my back, it was over and out as far as I was concerned. Do I need to remind you of the country hotel weekend break for three, where I discovered the two of you wrapped around each other and canoodling in the king-size four-poster? As Marjorie Proops once wrote to a woman unfortunate enough to have been in my position, one expects such faithlessness from men, but from a woman friend, never! The reason I was tense at his funeral was because it reminded me of *your* betrayal, not his.

As for me now being able to move on in life and missing lots of chances, may I remind you that the only reason that that 'nice Italian policeman' (incidentally, they are called *carabinieri* in their language – so named because of their rifles – you'd know that if you'd paid more attention to the culture of the countries we passed through, instead of singing 'Viva Espagna' and 'The Chicken Song' at every bar and disco you could find that served baked beans on toast) – where was I? Oh, yes . . . The only reason he became interested in me was because I had to flutter my lashes at him to stop you being shot. You had had far too much to drink and you were driving at twice the speed limit down the *autostrada* with a paper bag over your head, because, you said (or screamed, as I remember), you 'couldn't stand the sight of me any more'. Likewise the mechanic had to be mollified because we hadn't enough money to pay him for the repairs. If you call that, or similar, 'moving on in life' I don't wonder you are now living in a caravan park. And speaking of which, I don't know why you want me to correspond with you care of Audrey. If you think for one minute that I would visit you if you gave me your address, then you obviously didn't understand a single word of my letter.

Last, and by no means least, I don't know where you get the idea that Ida's husband is a transvestite. He wears bells on his trousers and a funny hat because he is a Morris dancer and that is all. Perhaps you have been hanging around Sheepdipper's for too long.

I notice you don't thank me for laundering your smalls, or for the fudge, but perhaps you are sent such gifts every day of the week and therefore don't think it worthy of comment.

I was very sorry to read of the fate of the previous

incumbent of your caravan. As you say, that poor woman's tragedy is your gain – but then that seems to be how life goes for you, doesn't it? I shall think of you when you are moving into your new home, and hope that all goes well.

Happy paddling.

Kind regards,

Irene

Tuesday

Dear Audrey,

I hope you don't mind being a 'poste restaurante', but Vera asked me to write to her c/o you. Would you mind very much giving her the enc. missive?

I hope you have been having jolly times together. She is great fun, of course, and so brave, considering what she has to put up with. I don't know whether she has told you, since she is the last one to ask for sympathy, but her only son is 'gay' and her daughter is a single mother, so it's hardly surprising she sometimes needs the solace of another woman's husband or lover. It's so sad to think that her memory is going. She told me in her last letter that she hadn't known her daughter was tattooed, but Karen has had 'Mum' on one hand and 'Hate' on the other for ages since.

I know I can rely on your discretion not to spread any of this around, now that she is trying to 'move on in life' and make her new home in your town.

Hope you are keeping well.

Kindest regards,

Irene Spencer

Lodge 202
Far Shores Trailer Park
Vicker-upon-St Agnes

Thursday

Irene,

It has come to my ears that you have been spreading malicious gossip about me. Audrey Roscoe popped down to the park this afternoon to tell me herself. Apparently my children are 'odd' as the result of an abusive childhood, my grandchild is illegitimate and my husband died in mysterious circumstances after learning I was a serial adulterer.

Speaking of which, you are someone to complain of 'wild and inaccurate observations'! My so-called 'affair' with Bill Snapes is a total ligament of your imagination. As I think I told you at the time, our being in bed together was a mistake from start to finish. There I was, as I thought, on a weekend break you had booked for you, me and Bill as three 'swinging singles', and I find myself in the Honeymoon Suite with a man I've barely been introduced to. (Though come to think of it, I could say the same for the first night I spent with my husband Gerald.) It was all your fault for booking the blithering Honeymoon Suite to begin with! It had more doors than a French farce. What with the separate bath-rooms, walk-in wardrobes and dimness of lighting, it's a wonder Bill and I found our way to the bed at all. As it was a 'King-size', we were peacefully slumbering at either side, without even knowing the other was there. I don't know which of the three of us was the more surprised when we woke up and found you wedged between us. I can recall to this day your fury. You were white-faced even through your make-up.

You tried to pass it off as a mistake the hotel had made, but who goes to bed in false eyelashes and bright pink lipstick, except in an advert? It was quite clear you had intended all along to end up in the bridal suite with Bill, and only the lateness of your train meant I got there before you.

Fortunately this is all *de rigueur* in a trailer park. If anything, it has raised my profile. I saw several people in the communal facilities pointing and staring with awe on their faces. (On reflection, that could have been owing to the state of my undies. The ones you returned are a violent shade of puce. Did you wash them with the beetroot borscht sheets? The fudge, by the way, finally put paid to my dentures. On contact with it, the Bostick melted.)

But – as I was saying – although it makes little difference here, apart from a visit from Victim Support and an invitation to bare all in the local paper, I don't want this outrageous slander all over St Agnes! I dread to think what could have happened if that letter had got into the wrong hands. I'm at a loss to understand your motives. All I have ever tried to be is a friend to you.

As such, I have discussed your perfidy with Site Security. Audrey got it wrong – this accommodation is not sheltered, it is 'protected' and he says for a small sum *he* will pay *you* a visit.

Yours,

Vera

PS His name is Damon, but not for nothing is he known as 'Demon'. The last person who caused bother to a resident is still in traction.

Lodge 202
Far Shores Trailer Park
Vicker-upon-St Agnes

Thursday

Dear Howard,

Sorry to be a bother, but could you return that £250 I lent you to install the Jacuzzi? I wouldn't ask you unless it was a matter of urgent family honour.

Mother

The Limes

Saturday

Dear Vera,

I don't know what to make of the wild and ridiculous assertations in your last, but I believe I have mentioned before about what an old stirrer Audrey Roscoe is. I have certainly never ever told anybody that the circumstances of Gerald's death were 'mysterious'. How could I, when I didn't even know myself until you just told me in your letter?

I will certainly not stoop to address your 'false memory syndrome' about our so-called 'three-in-a-bed' situation with Bill Snapes. Suffice it to say *I* thought it was buried in the past, but obviously you still enjoy getting it out for further inspection and rejigging of facts.

As for threatening me with a gorilla attack from a hired assassin, I can only think that you have embraced the lurid ethos of the trailer park you talk so proudly of with eager arms. Do not for one moment think that I am frightened by these scare tactics – I am merely hurt to have my friendship so rebuffed.

Goodbye, and good luck with the rest of your life,

Irene Spencer

The Limes

Saturday

Dear Lesley,

I have been thinking about you so much lately, and realise that it is selfish of me to let a little thing like fear of flying put me off visiting you in Melbourne. I don't wonder you have begged me to come out there on a visit so many times – it must be difficult now Keith has left you and you are having to juggle the demands of motherhood with working for your living. And if I don't come soon, little Cheryl Marie won't know her dear old Granny Spencer!

I have been looking into the rigmarole of getting a flight and insurance and applying for a visa and sorting things out this end so I can come for a good long stay, and find that unfortunately I won't be able to be with you before this coming Wednesday.

All my love, dear,

Mummy xxx

Far Shores Trailer Park

Tuesday

Dear Irene,

Can you ever forgive me? I don't know what came over me. Trailer-park dementia is the only excuse I can offer. I'm afraid they all watch far too many hysterical TV soaps and then tailor their lives accordingly. The stories I could tell you, and I've only been here a fortnight! My next-door neighbour, Yasmin, has had her patio dug up three times by police looking for parts of her common law husband. She says she wouldn't mind them finding him, he still owes her £48.50, but I presume she means in one piece, alive and kicking – which by all accounts he did frequently. Speaking of kicking, from the couple on the other side I hear constant screaming and shouting. One night I could stand it no more and went round to beg them to stop. I found him handcuffed to the bunk bed and her, dressed head to toe in black PVC, slapping him about with a fish slice. This was an unexpected view of marital abuse, but when I threatened to call social services they laughed. Apparently they were making material for 'surfers' to 'download' from the 'net'. They explained I was now on video and if I wanted to stay and join in they'd split the proceeds with me. There must be quite a taste for this sort of thing, they've got a socking great Mercedes parked outside. Which reminds me, I must tell Howard . . .

But I digress. I am really writing to apologise for my

threatening letter and, even worse, for following it up
in reality. Imagine my surprise and distress when
Damon returned with the news that the house was
locked and shuttered and the neighbours had told him
you had fled the country! As he said himself, there was
no need for that. He has 'nuff respec' for someone of
your great age and the most he would have done was
'trash' your flower beds. He's actually rather sweet and
most days pops round to check I'm all right and collect
his five pounds. Yesterday he offered to pierce my
navel. I'm sure it was kindly meant and not because I
didn't have any change on me.

I have just realised I have no idea where to send this.
Where are you, Irene? Perhaps you're scared to tell me,
but you need have no fear of further reprisals. I couldn't
possibly afford to give Damon another £250. Well, I will
address it to your former home in the hopes somebody
knows your whereabouts. Oh – I can see the postman
hovering the other side of the barbed wire. He won't
deliver on the site because of Damon's pit bull terrier.

Later:
The post brought a card from Karen telling me you
have gone to Australia! This was followed by a tirade
of abuse which, I presume, blames me. But I've
suffered so many over the years that as soon as I got to
'selfish, thoughtless, vile, ignorant, etc., etc.' I ceased
reading. No address, so I shall stick to plan A. Damon
will chase down the postman. He has a Countryman
Range Rover with four-wheel drive and bullbars,
which I think is a charming image in a trailer park.

I do hope this finds you, my dear, and that all is not

lost. I understand you can wander for days in the Outback, with only 'swaggermen' and dingoes for company.

Once more, many apologies and all my love,

Vera

19 Byron Street,
St Urban
Melbourne
VICTORIA

Monday

Dear Vera,

Your letter has finally caught up with me and I have paid the excess postage it cost to send it on here. Fortunately, since it only contained one sheet of paper and 'all your love' it didn't weigh very much.

I have thought long and hard as to whether to reply, but then I remembered it was coming up to your birthday (at least if you're posting from Australia), so I have decided to risk it and send you a card. If you've been threatening all your friends with bodily harm lately, it may be the only one you get. I note you still don't enclose your full address, so I shall have to send it to the trailer park and hope it finds you. I can hardly credit the life you describe there, and only hope you are happy at last to have found your level.

I am having a wonderful time here with my daughter, Lesley, and am so glad to be able to spend so much 'quality time' with my little granddaughter, Cheryl Marie. I really don't know how Lesley managed without me. It must be heart-breaking for you missing your own granddaughter's childhood, what with you being constantly at loggerheads with Karen. She wrote me a lovely long letter the other week, incidentally, full of fun as usual. She's thinking of coming out here on a visit.

I hope you won't be too lonely spending your birthday on your own, but at least on your caravan site it won't be dull, by the sounds of it. Karen told me that she definitely wouldn't be spending it with you this year (she phrased it rather differently, actually, but that was the gist), and she didn't think Howard and Antony would be either. Actually Lesley and I will be going to a beach barbecue with some friends on the day itself, so I will raise a glass of chilled 'Yarrunga Field' to wish you well.

All for now, as I must trot off and pick up Cheryl Marie from kindergarten and get something for our tea. Poor Lesley is worked off her feet at the estate agency, and has to spend an incredible amount of evenings dining with clients – she often gets home after midnight quite exhausted, poor lamb.

Happy birthday.

Regards,

Irene

Lodge 202
Far Shores Trailer Park
Vicker-upon-St Agnes

Sunday

Dearest Irene,

How wonderful to hear from you after all this time.
I thought you were dead. Perhaps savaged by kangaroos. I saw a programme on Discovery about them
and apparently they can turn quite nasty. Trust Karen
not to tell me she has been corresponding with you all
this time! She was always very secretive when she
was a child. I only found out she knew about babies
(though, in the light of events, clearly not enough) by
reading her diary.

Thank you for the birthday greetings – sweet of you
to remember. Personally, I'd rather not at my age. But
this year I didn't have a choice. Yasmin and Carol – did
I mention her? She's the one who's involved in 'net'
mail order videos – decided to give me a party. Yasmin
does tarot readings, so of course she knew the date and
she'd arranged a wonderful surprise with all the park
residents. She'd even invited Howard and Karen –
needless to say, their names had come up in my reading – Howard as the Hanging Man and Karen as the
Death card.

The whole of the park was decorated with bunting
– I later found out Yasmin's children had 'borrowed' it
from the promenade – and there was a fabulous
barbecue on *our* beach. It was a chilly night but it

warmed up when we roasted half a cow and twenty pounds of sausages. Carol's got an arrangement with the local butcher, something to do with the videos. Of course 'hooch' from Dave and Barbra's 'still' helped. They make a fiery concoction in an old tin bath in the lean-to which used to house their Elsan. The only thing that was 'chilled' (in Damon's parlance) at my barbecue was the guest list. In fact the party was 'kicking', to use the word for once in a less unpleasant connotation. Karen never appeared, which was a pity as Yasmin had offered a forecast. I forecast she wouldn't come, which hardly makes me psychic. But, despite a breakdown – possibly the car or possibly Antony, who was in tears – Howard and Antony arrived in time for the fireworks, a stunning display of Damon's home-made pyrotechnics. Speaking of 'bangers', the site is littered with them. Several flew through the air, along with Howard's toupee and the remains of the cow. Howard is now thinking of employing Damon for his Millennium bash, as he can always lay his hands on Semtex.

I'm so looking forward to the millennium. Yasmin has prophesied a high time here. I prophesy it will be in more ways than one if Damon has anything to do with it! Have you made any plans yet? What exactly *is* the religion in Australia?

Anyway, my dear, I'm baby-sitting Yasmin's children while she takes part in a 'Mystic Fayre'. I won't get a word written there – I need both hands free for them – so I'll finish.

Oh, Irene, I *have* missed your letters. I've told every-one here so much about you, Yasmin could do you an absent reading! Do keep in touch now, I'm longing to hear more about your life in Oz.

Love,

Vera

Down Under

Tuesday night, or is it Wednesday morning?

Dear Vera,

Thank you for your vivid account of your birthday celebrations – it sounded very pleasant if that is your preference for conviviality. It has been my birthday today – don't feel guilty about not sending a card whatever you do, it really couldn't matter less – and I have had the most wonderful time sampling the fruits of the New World vineyards. To make up for me having to baby-sit tonight while she, poor love, had to go to dinner with yet another client, Lesley bought me a case of Victorian wines all to myself. That's wines made in the state of Victoria, by the by, not during the late Queen's reign – took me a while to work that one out. I may be a little tipsy, so please excuse the writing.

Now to satisfy your curiosity about Australia. It is very big for starters, and very far away from everywhere else. The flight over is horrendous – a whole day in the air, can you imagine? – with a couple of hours off for good behaviour in Bangkok airport. You have your dinner and then watch two films and then go to sleep (those who can relax enough to do so) and then have breakfast, and then you look out of the window (those who are brave enough to do so) and see Australia, and then you keep flying across it for hours and hours and hours before you get to Melbourne, which is where Lesley moved to after she split up with Keith, and where there are no kangaroos, incidentally, and no dingoes either, fortunately for little Cheryl Marie.

Here, you have to think of everything upside down.
A north-facing garden means as much to them as a
south-facing one does to us, being in the other hemi-
sphere. Melbourne is down south and Melburnians are
very proud of their weather. They will tell you, at the
drop of a hat, that they can have all four seasons in any
given day. Depending on which way the wind blows, it
can bring the chill of the Antarctic or the heat of the
countryside (or 'bush' as they call it here). Today, for
example, I set off for a stroll along the beach in glorious
sunshine, only to be hit by hailstones the size of tennis
balls on the way back. Believe me, a parasol is no
defence against Antarctic ice.

But speaking of tennis balls, I must tell you about the
Sausage Sizzle I went to at the weekend, held by the
local tennis club to attract 'veterans' to start going to
play in the afternoons. Of course I hadn't been in
whites for many a long year, but fortunately there was
a group of novices like myself so I joined their number.
There was one lady there who reminded me of you,
actually – very jolly, but my, she suffered in the heat
with all her bulk. Anyway, there was a lovely man
there called Vincent – retired, a widower, very nicely
turned out and with a full head of hair and beautifully
shaped hands. I think even his teeth are his own. As
things fell out, we partnered each other most of the
afternoon and got on very well, and though Lesley's
house is really not far from the club, he insisted on
giving me a lift home. When it emerged in casual
conversation that it was going to be my birthday in a
couple of days, he suggested he take me out to lunch.
(Actually, he suggested dinner, but what with Lesley's

busy schedule I knew I couldn't count on having the night off.) Which is where I've been today. He'd booked us into a very exclusive restaurant at the harbour with a wonderful view and no expense spared. I had oysters, crayfish and three kinds of chocolate mousse, and it was superb. It was so lovely to have the company of a man again, and he's so much better looking than Bill. Unfortunately he has to visit his grandchildren for a few days now, but we've arranged to play tennis again next Wednesday.

Just got up to let Lesley in, and fell down. All now. Bit tiddly. Tell more about Australia next time. Felt all right before, but standing was mistake. Remind me to tell you about the possum.

Love from your pal,

Inebriated Irene (joke – ha ha!) xxxxxx

Lodge 202 etc.

Friday

My dear Irene,

How remiss of me to forget your birthday! Really, sometimes I wonder if Karen isn't right about the state of my brain, though it goes against the grain to admit it. Enclosed is a Birthday Tarot from Yasmin, which I gave her all the data to prepare. Funnily enough I remembered that perfectly! I had to guess the time of birth of course, but I do recall you telling me your mother cursed you for arriving when she was at her lowest ebb, so I imagine that was about four in the morning.

Yasmin also brought this little news article which, having done your reading, she thought might be of interest. Perhaps you had better show it to 'Vincent'! (Keep on with the booze, then you won't go all buttoned up on him – men like a chatty woman.) Oz really does sound like the land of change. Especially the weather.

Talking of hailstones, I am off to Sheepdipper's for the weekend. It's Howard and Antony's anniversary and they are having a 'Do'. Howard wants a hand with the catering – plenty of sizzling sausages – it's a Fork and Finger event.

There's life in us old girls yet, eh? Promise to write fully on my return.

Love,

Vee

PS Don't forget the possum!

Vicker-upon-St Agnes *Star*

The secret to a long and healthy life is SEX! Sex keeps people young and vibrant and halts the ageing process, according to Dr Raj Garibaldi, who insists, 'Ageless national icons like Margaret Thatcher and the Queen Mother are leading very vigorous sex lives.'

St Urban

Tuesday

Dear Vera,

Sorry it's been a few weeks since writing. I'm afraid in the interim I've mislaid your last letter, so I can't remember if there were any questions therein. I do seem to remember you appeared to be obsessed with sex, which is a shame in an older person, I always think, and more often seems to afflict the men, as in 'dirty old' etc. Have you started back on the UHT again, I wonder? I really don't think it suits you.

Thank you for the Birthday Tarot reading from your new friend Yasmin (is that a Romany name?), which I found today at the back of my underwear drawer. I didn't know they needed birth dates and times for the cards – I thought that was Astrology? Anyway, if they do and if it is important to the accuracy, that explains why it makes no sense to me at all – you've got my birth year down so wrong that I'd be eighty-three! Was that your little joke or her bad handwriting? Certainly I have never seen myself as having a 'burning, passionate nature, hidden beneath a cool exterior which aches to be torn down'. I would consider myself to be almost the opposite, in fact – at least as far as any tearing down goes. At any rate, I can see what Karen means about your memory.

Did I mention in my last that I have joined a tennis club? I now play two afternoons a week, partnered by a charming gentleman called Vincent. He is a widower, very fit and active for his years, with a full head of hair and all his own teeth. He used to be in hosiery, I believe. Imagine my surprise when he insisted on taking me out to lunch on my birthday! We went to a very exclusive harbourside restaurant and ate oysters and crayfish and three kinds of wine (including a champagne), one to go with each course. The wine here is very good – much better than European. Lesley bought me a mixed case for my birthday as an intro-duction to New World vinny culture, but there seem to be so many to learn! On the couple of occasions that I've managed to get a Sunday off (Lesley works most weekends and so I usually look after Cheryl Marie), Vincent has driven me out to local vineyards for tast-ings and lunch, and I have availed myself of his having a four-wheel drive to buy several cases to sample at my leisure.

It's no use. I've got to stop. The ruddy possum is at it again and I just can't concentrate for the racket. Remind me to tell you about it another time.

Write soon,

Irene

Lodge 202
Far Shores Trailer Park
Vicker-upon-St Agnes

Thursday . . . or Friday

Dear Irene,

I started a letter to you ages ago but I've quite
forgotten where I put it. Incidentally, you did mention
Vincent, the tennis club, the teeth, the lunch, the
oysters, the crayfish and the wine in your last one.
Perhaps you should go easy on the New World 'vinny
culture' – is that an Australian expression?

Wrong date or not, I thought Yasmin's description of
you was completely accurate, though she did mention
part of your trouble was accepting it. Where on earth
do you get the idea that I am sex-obsessed? I haven't
given it a thought in days, and no, I'm not on UHT,
but I'm sure this genetically modified food has a lot to
answer for. Howard won't touch it. He insists it has
the opposite effect to increasing sex drive and in fact
may be leading to the men growing breasts and wanting to have babies.

Which reminds me, I was writing to you about his
'Do', which gave a whole new meaning to 'fork and
finger'. I didn't know it was possible to attach so much
metal to body parts. One of his guests appeared to be
wearing an entire canteen of cutlery. Outside of a boot
fair, I've never seen so much fingering in public – and
as for the 'sizzling sausages'! Clearly no one there was
eating GM foods, though of course, being Howard's,

there was plenty of soya. I'm still shockable, it seems, despite everything we see nowadays on television.

The most important news is that Karen was there with her little girl, Sabrina. It was the first time I'd seen them in over a year, and my, how Sabrina has grown. She is a charming little thing and soon got used to calling me Granny. When I arrived she didn't seem to know who I was, and asked if it was me who Mummy called 'the mad old bat'. When Karen heard I was living in a trailer park, she laughed raucously and said I'd graduated from soap opera to cartoon, whatever that means. Anyway, being homeless again she decided to come and stay, though of course I pointed out that space was limited.

The first morning was very awkward. I'd put up a curtain to give her some privacy, but she still sleeps till lunchtime and I needed to get to the kitchenette, so I popped my head round and asked if she wanted some 'brunch'. She swore loudly and said, 'Give me a chance to put my knickers on before you start stuffing food down me.' I admit I was hurt. I said, 'I don't seem to be able to do a thing right these days,' to which she responded, 'Crashing in on a person when they're half-naked is never "right", Mother, and you've been doing it for sixty-five years.' She is as rude as ever and, besides, how does she know? I've only been doing it to her for thirty-five of them. This morning she staggered up and snapped off my favourite classical music radio programme, saying it 'did her head in'. She's been here a month and if she doesn't go soon, it will do *my* head in.

How do you manage with Lesley? Perhaps it's easier

because she's out all the time. Whatever kind of a job requires seven days a week? I hope she is getting good bonuses. I'd be glad if Karen got any job at all. My pension won't stretch to the luxuries she demands. She's just given me a list which includes Java coffee beans, gravadlax, luxury shower gel and a mobile phone. I shall have to speak to Damon.

All for now – it's time to pick Sabrina up from school. She is lodging next door with Carol and Terry.

Write soon, I need support!

Lots of love,

Vera

PS What on earth's going on with the possum?

St Urban
Australia

Dear Vera,

Thank you for your newsy letter. I won't bother to tell you any more about my lovely outings with Vincent if it causes offence, and I do so apologise, I'm sure, if I've been boring you with my repetition. (By the by, speaking of which, although you claim not to be obsessed with 'sex', I notice you managed to cram it in twice in one paragraph.) I can't imagine where you get the idea that my repeating myself has anything to do with drink, as I am just a social drinker, as you well know. It's simply old age and can't be helped. As I keep having to explain to Lesley, 'Wait till it happens to you!' I only wish I could be there to say, 'I told you so,' when her little brain isn't as sharp as it is now.

How funny that we're both involved in looking after our grandchildren at the moment. Having children is much nicer the second time round, don't you find? Or maybe it's just that Cheryl Marie is an easier child than Lesley was. Incidentally, you ask what type of job she has, although I'm sure I've mentioned several times (perhaps *you're* the one who's drinking too much and killing off brain cells!). She is an estate agent, and things are done very differently here in Australia as far as house sales go. Instead of making individual appointments for buyers to see properties, they have an open time at weekends. The owner has to leave for an hour or so, while one of the agents shows people round and gives the patter, so here they really work for their commission. Also, nearly all properties are auctioned, not just the ones that are falling down and hard to get rid of like in England, so Saturdays and Sundays Lesley's either showing houses or out selling them under her hammer. The auctions are held outside the property in the street and are quite exciting. Usually they have a dummy bidder just to start the ball rolling, and my services have been called upon in this respect a couple of times. I felt almost as nervous as if I was really buying!

You ask me to tell you about the possum, but I'm sure I already have. When you see them in the garden they're really very sweet, so you wouldn't mind them living in the attic if it wasn't for them doing their 'business' through the ceiling . . .

You wouldn't believe it, just as I was writing about it! You'd almost think they could read your thoughts. Right on my head this time, and all over this letter! Well, I'm sorry, I haven't got time to write it out again – this is already my fair copy. I've dabbed it with kitchen paper and that will have to do. It's just lucky I'm using Biro instead of pen and ink. And now I shall have to shampoo my hair before picking up little Cheryl Marie from school, and ring Pete the Possum up again to make another appointment, and scrub the sofa and rug. And here I am supposed to be enjoying my retirement and being cosseted a bit myself in my old age! A woman's work is never done, Vera, particularly if she is a grandmother!

Do give Karen my love, and tell her I'll be replying to her letter soon. What a pity you haven't been getting on better. She's such a lovely girl. Isn't it great that she and Damon seem to be hitting it off?

All for now. Take care.

Love,

Irene xx

Lodge 202
Far Shores Trailer Park
Vicker-upon-St Agnes

Monday

Dear Irene,

I didn't know a thing about Karen and Damon
'hitting it off' until Karen announced they were going to
St Tropez for the weekend. Apparently Damon has associates in protection on a caravan site there. I was, to coin
one of her phrases, 'gobsmacked'. Needless to say, I was
expected to look after Sabrina. Not that it was any hard-
ship – she really is delightful. I can always get a cuddle
from her. Karen was such an unrewarding child in that
department. She would go as stiff as a board whenever
I attempted to touch her. I can only assume Damon
does not encounter the same problem.

I've taken advantage of her absence to move Sabrina
in with me. To be honest, I'd become a little concerned at
her boarding with Carol and Terry, what with them
being in the sex video business. Sabrina kept appearing
with new shoes and chocolate, and one hears such terrible things nowadays. Besides, I just couldn't stand
having Karen as a guest a moment longer. She has
turned my little dwelling upside down, just when I'd
got it how it suits me. When she returns (if she ever does
– they went for three days and have already been gone a
fortnight) she will have to make her own arrangements.
Perhaps, given her history, *she* should move in with
Carol and Terry.

I have now reorganised the space so Sabrina has her

own little bedroom and play area, and without Karen's fourteen boxes of cosmetics – including a do-it-yourself piercing kit – I can now get into my own bathroom! I'm considering getting an extension built on. Dave next door but one has offered to do it. My days revolve around Sabrina's needs, and I admit it's given me a new lease of life. Howard always said I was lost if I couldn't be a carer. I think that nice Jack Straw is right about appointing surrogate grannies. Perhaps his own childhood was deprived of one.

By the way, I know what you mean about 'business'. What with the dogs, cats, goats and chickens, the site is littered with it. The other day Sabrina came in and said she'd been playing 'marbles'. Imagine my disgust when I found they were dried rabbit pellets!

Friday

Karen returned, very brown, last night, and informed me she was moving in with Damon. On reflection I am not surprised. They are two of a kind. Especially in their tastes. They came back with the Range Rover stacked with booze and his and her Rolex watches. She wants Sabrina to move in with them. Over my dead body.

Must stop – it's Sabrina's bath time, then I read her a story. When she arrived, all her books were about one-parent families and children brought up by 'same-sex couples'. We're so enjoying *The Wind in the Willows*.

Huggies, as Sabrina says,

Vee

PS I enclose a photo of Sabrina and me taken by Carol. Do send some of you and Cheryl Marie. And the possum!

St Urban
Australia

Sunday

Dear Vera,

Thank you for your last. I notice you started it on the
Monday and finished it on the Friday. Is that because it
was an awful chore, or did you mislay it? I hope it was
the latter, although I wouldn't wish memory loss on
anybody, not even my worst enemy. You'd think I was
gaga the way Lesley goes on when I can't think of a
word.

And speaking of gaga, how on earth can you
compare possum piddle to rabbit pellets? Do you think
we have a hole in the ceiling for it to pooh through? Its
Number Ones came dripping down on my head when I
was writing last time, not its Number Twos. I can't
believe I'm having to write this and be so explicit. Trust
you. We've had Pete the Possum round twice now, but
it just seems to find its way in again. They put a trap in
the attic with a bit of apple as bait. You know when it's
been caught, because it bangs the cage about like billy-o.
The first time it happened I thought we'd got burglars
and I phoned the police – I did feel a fool!

Thank you for the photograph of Sabrina. What a
sweet little girl she's proving to be, and so like her
Granny Small – she certainly got your nose! Here's one
of Cheryl Marie taken at a fancy dress. She's the one
dressed as Little Bo Peep. She's such a little actress and
yet so practical! See how she's taken the telescope from

Captain Cook to look for her sheep. (Captain Cook was the Englishman who discovered Australia, but if you ask me it couldn't have been very difficult. After all, the Aborigines had already been living there for thousands of years, so they must have found it easily enough.)

I've just returned from another wonderful day out with Vincent. He's such a lovely man and such good company. He won't let me do a thing for myself when we're together – he even opens the car door for me and makes sure I'm settled nicely before he goes all the way round to get in himself. The only time Clive did that was once when we were courting, and then he slammed the door on my leg. Vincent keeps talking about us going away for a weekend, but I don't know how Lesley would manage without me if we did. She's out at work so much, poor dear, that we hardly ever see each other – we communicate by notes. It's not so much like having a daughter, it's more like having another pen-pal!

I had a super postcard from Karen from St Tropez telling me all about her exciting news. I bet you can't wait, and Sabrina must be over the moon! I often worry about Cheryl Marie, being an only. Lesley was, of course, and I'm afraid she got very spoilt as a result. Don't be worried about Damon being wayward – as I said to Karen in my last, this might be just the thing to settle him down.

All for now. Hope this finds you as it leaves me – pleasantly exhausted after a thoroughly enjoyable day.

Fondest thoughts,

Irene

Lodge 202
Far Shores Trailer Park

Friday

Dear Vera . . . I mean Irene,

I'm so upset I've forgotten my own name now!
Thank you for informing me in your last of Karen's
'exciting news'. It was certainly more than *she* had
bothered to do. Odd to be told of your daughter's preg-
nancy via Australia when she is living twenty yards
away. We have the speed of technology to thank for
that, I suppose. Thank goodness I don't have e-mail, or
I could have known before she did!

She hasn't spoken to me since I confronted her with
your letter, but Sabrina came back from school
demanding a home computer, so I've had to communicate with Damon. He's as pleased as a pit bull terrier
with two tails. He's already making a list of names and
has started to call me Mother.

I hope this *doesn't* find you as it leaves me – hurt and
confused.

Yours,

Irene . . . I mean Vera!

Saturday

Dear Howard,

I am writing to tell you, since I'm sure Karen won't – really, when I think of the money I've wasted on joined-up-writing tuition! – that we are to have an addition to the family. You will soon be the proud uncle of a boy called Dale or Liam or Vinny. I dread to think what the poor mite will be named if she's a girl, but Damon doesn't entertain the possibility.

I only found out by a chance remark from Irene. Proof, as ever, that Karen cuts me cruelly out of her life. It'll be a different story when she wants baby clothes or a baby-sitter.

Sorry, dear, if I'm sounding depressed. Sometimes I think the world has changed in such a bewildering way, I no longer feel a part of it.

Hope you and Antony are happy at least, with the sheep.

Mumsie

Monday

Dear Ms Matthews,

I understand from my granddaughter, Sabrina Small, that, to keep abreast of her studies, she must have a 'state-of-the-art' computer with built-in modem, fax and heliport. I am an OAP on an inadequate fixed income (has Tony Blair considered people like us in his enthusiasm for 'IT', I wonder?), and I'm at a loss to know where to turn. Are there any grants available?

Yours sincerely,

Vera Small

Thursday

Dear Vera,

I'm very worried about you – you seem absolutely distraught! In fact you must be, to send me all your other correspondence in your last. I'm sending back the enc., because I don't know Sabrina's school's address, but I've forwarded Howard's letter on to him at Sheepdipper's. I've also taken the liberty of writing a little note to Karen, in the hope of pouring oil on troubled waters.

Now come on, chin up, look at the positive – I've been reading all about it in one of Lesley's many self-help books that she bought when she was going through the divorce. You count your blessings – write them down. You'll be surprised how they add up!

Oh dear, I was going to help by starting a list, but it's time for tennis, so you'll have to do it on your own. Probably more therapeutic, anyway.

Cheerio for now, and get on with that list!

Sending love and encouraging thoughts,

Irene xx

19 Byron Street
St Urban
Melbourne

Thursday

Dear Howard,

Your mother sent the enc. to me in error, so by the time you get this, what with the post, she'll have been waiting a couple of weeks for a reply. She seems in a terrible state, and I really think she needs a break from trailer park life. Couldn't you and Antony have her to stay for a little holiday? I know she can be difficult, but I do think it sounds like a real cry for help, don't you? Would you let me know how she seems when you see her?

Fondest regards, and also to Antony,

Irene Spencer

Thursday

Dear Karen,

Here at last are the bootees I promised. I made them in unisex yellow, as you can see. I told your Mum about the baby, as you asked, and you were right – it did come as a bit of a shock, but I'm sure inside she's as thrilled as you are. I think it might have helped if you'd told her that you and Damon were an 'item', as you call it, from the start. I think she thought of him as *her* special friend – she often mentioned him in her letters – so there may have been a little bit of jealousy there. Just a thought.

Anyway, dear, I know you try to be kind and patient with her. And of course I don't think you were selfish to move out of the caravan and leave her on her own. I spent several weeks cooped up in a Dormobile with her when we toured the Continent, don't forget, and I thought I'd end up in the funny farm!

Take care, and love to Damon,

Lots of love and hugs,

Rene xxx

Middle Parks
Middle Piddle
Worcs.

Wed.

Dear Irene,

Enjoying a few days at magical Middle Parks. It was Sabrina's half-term and what with everything I felt I needed a break, so I cashed in a little insurance policy and we just took off. Sabrina is having a fine old time with all the activities, and I am basking in the indoor 'sun', so much more reliable than the real thing and, I believe, less damaging. You would know all about that in Australia, of course – doesn't it hold the world record for skin cancer? Hope you are not economising with the sun block on your tennis outings. One looks a fool with all those white stripes, but better safe than sorry.

You've probably written in reply to my last so this may cross with it, but I just wanted to put your mind at rest that I'm feeling much better, what with the aromatherapy massage (Yasmin's instructions) and leisurely drinks round the pool. Just popped on a sarong – I'm sure you've discovered them, so comfortable – to go for one now. A charming widower here has invited me for 'tropical cocktails'.

I enclose a couple of postcards so you can see the luxuriant foliage.

Love, and thanks for being a good, albeit distant, friend.

Vera

Dear Howard,

Just a quick postcard from our lovely residence. I never imagined a 'log cabin' could be so comfortable. A huge bath and no need to wrestle with gas cylinders. I could stay here for ever.

Sabrina sends love, as I do,

Mumsie

Very late on Saturday night

Dear Vera,

Thank you for the postcard. I'm so relieved you seem to be feeling better – I was quite worried about you. Depression is an awful thing, isn't it? Or so I suppose – I've never suffered from it myself, fortunately.

Since I last wrote I have joined a creative writing class for senior citizens. It's funny, isn't it? I have to come to the other side of the world to do things that I could have been doing all along at home – playing tennis, penning poems – but one just doesn't seem to get round to it in the normal run of things. I suppose it is that, knowing so few people here, there aren't the usual distractions. Apart from looking after Cheryl Marie full-time, that is. Lesley's had to go away for a week on a course now. Her boss seems to think a great deal of her. He came to pick her up personally in his car to run her out to the airport.

I can't seem to get to sleep tonight, so I've been having a bit of fun alone, opening up a few bottles of the Victorian wine Lesley bought me, and doing blind tastings. I don't know if I'm getting any better at it – they all seem to taste nice to me – but it passes the time.

Oh, well. I'll try to sleep again. At this rate, Cheryl Marie will be up before I've gone to bed!

Hope you are still feeling the benefit of your holiday,

Fond regards,

Irene

PS Couldn't sleep, so penned this poem, enc.:

Reflections in the Dead of Night

a poem by
Irene Spencer

Looking up at the coal-black sky,
I see my life, and wonder why –
Why did I do this, why did I do that,
E.g., why did I buy that hat?

It looked so pretty in the shop,
With bows a-quiver, brim a-flop –
What happened on the way back home
To change it to a shapeless dome?

And isn't that a lot like life,
When you cut it apart with the surgeon's knife,
How oft do we rush after new fool's gold,
Instead of treasuring the trusty old?

Lodge 202
Far Shores Trailer Park

Saturday

Irene!

Arrived home to crossed letters and crossed wires!
What on earth did you say to Howard and Karen after
my confidential disclosures? Whatever it was has
released a maelstrom. Howard was convinced I had run
away to live in a log cabin. It was a 'cry for help' and I
was in a 'terrible state' as I am jealous of Karen's relationship with Damon. They all agreed I'd gone
completely round the twist and absconded with
Sabrina! I was lucky to escape arrest. They have had the
police out scouring the country and hourly bulletins on
National radio. It was only the peace and seclusion of
Middle Piddle that kept me from knowing about it.

I have explained to the police that I left a note under
the door of Damon's trailer, and his blasted pit bull
terrier must have chewed it, but they refuse to believe
me. They are now considering prosecution.

Judging by the doggerel you enclosed, I can only
assume you got carried away by the 'creative' side of
your writing. Either that or you have been indulging in
too many blind tastings. If this is what you call 'treasuring the trusty old' I'd rather not be one of them!

Karen is demanding I give Sabrina back, though she
of course wants to stay with me, and I am now to be
assessed by social workers. A Ms Clinch is coming to
make a 'home visit'.

Don't write again unless it is to offer something in mitigating circumstances.

Vera

dear Auntie Vera,

Granny is cryin all the time and drinkin a lot of pop. I have dawred you this picsure of you lookin cross, and she has writ you a pome. She is very sorry.

Love from

Cheryl Marie xxxxxxxxxxxxxxx

St Urbans
Melbourne
Australia

Dear Vera,

The Judgement Of The Damned

A poem by
Irene Spencer

One day – alas, 'twill be all too soon –
I will stand in the line to be judged:
To one side will go the souls that are clean,
To the other, the souls that are smudged.

As I shuffle along on penitent knees,
My head bowed before me in shame,
I will know that St Peter will turn me away,
For 'twas I who was wholly to blame.

'What is your crime?' my Maker will say,
His voice sending ice down my spine,
'Will you be going along with Old Nick,
Or are you a daughter of Mine?'

'I have sinned, Lord,' I'll say in a trembling voice,
'And must go to the fires of Hell.'
'Let me be the judge,' He'll say in fierce tone,
'Begin now, your story to tell.'

I'll tell Him of when I was far from home,
Of the letters that crossed on the sea,
Of the misunderstandings, the heartache I caused,
I will tell Him of Vera and me.

And when I am finished, the Lord's voice will lift
To Lucifer, Keeper of Hell,
'Forget it,' He'll say, 'she's coming with me,
For her "sin" was just loving too well.'

But alas that is fantasy, only a dream,
I am still in the state known as Life.
If only, my heart cries, my friend was like God,
Forgiving, and staying her knife.

I meant well, my friend, cannot mercy be mine?
Can I not make your heart feel a sway?
If sackcloth and ashes could undo the harm,
Dear Vera, I'd wear them each day.

With love from Irene (x?)

Far Shores Trailer Park

Monday

Dear Irene,

I was stunned by your recent missive. How long have you been having conversations with God? I showed it to my psychic next-door neighbour Yasmin, and she asked if you've ever thought of the 'laying on of hands'? I said that as far as I knew only on gullible widowers.

I don't know what to make of the sentiments expressed, but it's obvious to me that all this Australian wine-tasting you've spoken about has taken you over completely. If you really want help, get off the 'pop' and into the sackcloth and ashes.

Since you are on such intimate terms with God, *I* need you to intercede for *me*. Urgently. My fate is in His hands and your knees. The social worker, Ms Clinch, is paying her 'home visit' on Friday, and if we fail to live up to her expectations (whatever they may prove to be), she may take my granddaughter, Sabrina, away from me and give her back to her awful mother – or should I say, she who used to be known as my daughter, Karen?

Vera

PS In case God is deaf to your pleas, I have pinned up your verses to our notice-board. Hopefully they will frighten Ms Clinch into making the right decisions.

St Urban
Melbourne
Australia

Tuesday

Dear Vera,

I hope you don't mind me calling you that. I don't
think we've ever met, but my Mum, Irene, talks so
much about you that I feel I know you. I've been
having to deal with her mail recently, and your last
note sounded pretty urgent, so I thought I'd better
reply.

Mum has been under a bit of strain lately and I've
had to admit her to a private clinic I managed to find
upstate. Nothing major, just a little breakdown – you
know how nervy she can get. Maybe it's been too
much for her having to look after Cheryl Marie. I
don't know – you think you're doing her a favour,
making her feel needed, and then she pulls a stunt
like this. As it is, I had to take a couple of days off
work to sort everything out, and I've hired an au pair,
so when they let Mum out she'll be able to go back
home to England. I'll let you know when that is, as
I'm sure you'll want to pick her up from the airport,
you two being such old friends.

I'll pass on your letter when I next visit her if she's
up to focusing again, but they thought it might take a

little while for the hallucinations to stop, so personally I'm not holding my breath.

All the best,

Lesley Crabtree, née Spencer

Lodge 202
Far Shores Trailer Park

Saturday

Dear Lesley,

How nice to have personal contact with you at last
after all this time. Of course, I feel I know you well . . .
too well on occasions . . . from all your mother's
comments. But I'm sure in real life you are very different. Actually, we did meet once, at your wedding. You
looked magical in your Princess Di frock, all pink and
giggly. You may not remember, you were quite tipsy
from the wine – I understand from Irene you have a lot
of it in Oz, so I hope you still enjoy it as much as she
does. Anyway, it was a lovely occasion, though
perhaps, under the circumstances, you won't wish to
be reminded. It's so sad when marriages break up.
Your mother gave me a blow-by-blow account of yours.
All your psychiatric treatment and chanting and self-
help manuals! I know she was very concerned for you.
   Speaking of which, I'm so sorry to hear about Irene.
Whatever is the matter? Hallucinations?! I must admit,
looking back, her last few letters were rather odd.
Positively unhinged, in fact, especially the last one. Full
of wild 'poetic' ramblings. I understand some poets *are*
prone to hallucinations – Samuel Taylor Coleridge, for
example – but at least he wrote reasonable rhymes
when under the influence. Your mother's efforts would
have disgraced a Christmas cracker. In a way, it's a
relief to know she was 'on' something.

I blame myself, of course. I should have paid more attention. Friends can tell each other things they'd never admit to their daughters, and she might have confided her 'problem'. Where I wonder did she get hold of the 'substances'? Surely not at the tennis club?! Here, it would be no problem. A trailer park is like a pharmacy, except it doesn't stock hot-water bottles.

I've been having my own troubles with Health. In this case, Environmental. I won't bore you with the details – it's all to do with the suitability of my home for my own dear little granddaughter, Sabrina. Really, four fire extinguishers in fifteen square feet should be enough, but no – it's fireproof doors and fireproof sheets. . . . It's not as though Sabrina or I smoke in bed! A rather unpleasant Ms Clinch descended with her stormtroopers and stripped the place, looking for good-ness knows what. They went through Sabrina's hair for nits, made a list of the contents of the fridge and took a sample for 'analysis' from the toilet! You'd think that if a child was well fed, clean, happy and loved it would be enough, but not, it seems, compared to the contents of the Elsan. I haven't heard their decision yet, and I must say I'm living on the edge of an abyss. And I'm not talking about the Elsan.

Don't give Irene my last note – it might push *her* into one. I'm enclosing another, and a postal order for flow-ers – something pastel – which I'm sure you'll be kind enough to purchase. Do let me know how she goes on.

Best regards,

Vera

Dear Irene,

I am sorry to hear about your breakdown. Has God been appearing to you again? Or was it a 'contretemps' with your boyfriend, Vincent? I never felt right about him. He was altogether too good to be true. Especially the teeth. Anyone of that age who tells you they are his own is either a freak of nature or lying.

Lesley tells me you are coming home to England, and to be honest I'm glad. Australia's too far away, and, by the sound of it, dangerous. You will be fine once you are back. At least English madness is familiar.

Do write as soon as you can tell a pen from a knife.

All my love,

Vera

PS My psychic neighbour Yasmin says try to record your 'hallucinations'.

Room 101
Woolabulla WellBeing Clinic
Woolabulla

Dear Vera,

I am sneaking this out with someone who's leaving.
Please come and rescue me. I'm sure I shouldn't be in
here – everybody is mad. A woman with a nasty face
has visited me once, claiming to be my daughter. She
brought me some bright pink and purple flowers that
looked like ladies' unmentionables, and your note.
Who is she – is she one of Them? They give me pills
that make me feel funny, and one time tried to toast my
head in a machine. I'm not sure how long I've been
here, but I think it could be about ten years.

I am sending hallucinations for Yasmin in blank
poetry form (thankfully we have Creative Writing
Therapy here) – I hope she enjoys them better than me.
The drugs trolley is coming!!!! I've got to hide.

I'll expect you tomorrow. Bring wine.

Love,

Irene

PS Who is Vincent? Is he one of Them too?

Hallucinations for Yasmin

by
I. Spencer

Yellow men with funny fingers
Purple polyps on my nose
Frilly fringes in my eyebrow
Wires and spikes and all things nice
Rats as big as full moon craters
Leaving dentures on my bed
Howling winds and grinning mices
The cork's in the bottle!
The cork's in the bottle!
The cork's in the bottle and it can't get out!!!!!

Lodge 202/202½
Far Shores Trailer Park

Friday

Dear Lesley,

I received the most barmy note from Irene (enc.). I
showed it to my next-door neighbour Yasmin, a trained
psychic, and she said it's obvious Irene is on Planet
Zog. I don't know where that is, but if the hallucinations are anything to go by it must be very unpleasant.

I am now seriously worried about her condition. I
only wish I could come and get her, but I'm up to my
neck in plasterboard – all the fault of the
Environmental Dept – they've got a cheek, calling
themselves 'Health'.

I feel I should warn you, she seems to have taken
against you. Do be careful. She can be very aggressive,
as I know to my cost. There's only one way to deal
with her when she gets like this!

Fond regards,

Vera

Dear Irene,

Pull yourself together. You're behaving like a loony.
In fact, you are a loony. Never mind the pills – if you
carry on like this 'They' will have you in a strait-jacket.
Believe me, I know. The number of times Karen's tried
to have me Sectioned! In case you've forgotten, Karen
is my daughter and your friend. I have asked her to
write to you.

Looking back over our recent correspondence, it
occurs to me your troubles all come from the bottom of
a glass. Many bottoms. You, Irene, are an alcoholic.
There, I've said it.

Take the medication! It will return you to normal.
Well, as normal as can be expected. I'm sure you're
hiding it in very inventive places. I haven't forgotten
how cunning you were, when you fell out with my
cooking.

Try and focus on the good things in your life. Apart
from wine, that is. Above all, keep the cork in the
bottle!

Tough love,

Vera

PS I am enclosing a note from my psychic neighbour
Yasmin.

Running Water Lodge
Far Shores Trailer Park

Dear Irene,

I feel a ruby-red aura around you, which is causing
the distress. I shall send absent healing. Meanwhile,
meditate on the crystal enclosed and try rubbing it on
the polyps.

Yours in spirit,

Yasmin Brown
(spells, tarot and psychic counselling)

St Urban
Melbourne
Australia

Dear Vera,

Thanks for your letter of a few weeks ago and sorry I haven't replied sooner. The au pair I told you about proved to be a disaster, and I've had to take loads of time off work to look after my daughter, Cheryl Marie, myself.

I hope you don't mind, but I read the note you sent Mum. The alcoholic bit made a lot of sense to me – she drained a dozen bottles of wine I bought her for her birthday in a couple of days. Told me she'd spilt them! Anyway, it seemed to make sense to her too when she read it, and although it made her very upset at first, soon afterwards she seemed to pull herself together and make steady progress, which the Clinic were very pleased with. Until this latest bombshell happened.

The Clinic phoned last night to tell me Mum has gone missing. Apparently, a woman calling herself Karen turned up, claiming to be 'Irene's friend Vera's daughter'. She had a man with her that the manager described as a 'gorilla', called Damon, who wouldn't take no for an answer, so they were allowed in to visit her. The next thing the staff at the Clinic knew was that they had disappeared, apparently taking Mum with them. I don't mind – it was costing an arm and a leg to keep her in there, and apparently they were going to discharge her today anyway, but I just thought you should know.

Since I imagine they'll be taking her back to England, I've packed up the rest of Mum's things and shall be having them shipped across later in the week to her home address. Unfortunately, it's most of her clothes, and it'll take a couple of months to arrive, what with Customs checks in both countries. Anyway, if you hear from her before I do, will you tell her they're on their way?

Thanks for your help,

Irene's daughter, Lesley

The Outback

Thursday or Friday of this week

Dear Vera,

I'm free! Your daughter and son-in-law-to-be are my heroes! Feeling so much better, and am off the booze. Thank you for bringing me to my senses, old friend. Am still taking the tablets, which Karen managed to find in the clinic drugs trolley in a bottle labelled 'Irene Spencer' – talk about a coincidence! Anyway, they make me a bit tired and not quite sure of the date (see above) – but at least now I'm getting the week right!

Please thank your friend Yasmin for the absent healing, which seems to have worked a treat. I didn't know what to do with the crystal though – I've never had a polyp in my life, purple or otherwise.

Shall be coming home soon, but Damon said we should lie low for a while in case they've staked out the airports – sounds a bit paranoid to me! Still, he seems to know his way round a billycan, so we're living well, if rough. Karen is well. She's *so* pregnant and huge that we tell her she looks like the kangaroos, which at the moment are our nearest neighbours!

See you soon, I hope.

One step at a time.

I am an alcoholic . . . There, I've said it too!

Lots of love,

Irene

Lodge 202/203
Far Shores Trailer Park

Saturday

Dear Lesley,

I am sorry to trouble you again, especially at a time
when you're trying to find your feet as a mother, but I
wonder if you've heard from Irene yet? I've had these
last two letters (enc.) returned to me as 'Not known at
this address'. Of course, 'The Outback, Australia',
which is where she last wrote from, isn't much to go
on. I'm so angry with my daughter, Karen, and her
boyfriend, Damon. It's typical of their irresponsible
behaviour, though they've never gone as far as abduc-
tion before. If you had all her clothes, whatever is
Irene wearing? Surely she's not running round the
bush in a hospital nightgown? And I dread to think
what 'medication' they've got her on. Damon is probably growing it!

They left me in a terrible mess. Damon was half-way
through building an extension to my trailer. I had to
call in Dave from next-door-but-one, and he was horrified. Took the whole thing down and started again.
Said it was an accident waiting to happen, could have
caved in at any moment. Irene mentioned they are
'living rough'. I only hope Damon isn't exercising his
so-called building skills, or they may not live long
enough for me to see my new grandchild.

It's a pity you aren't enjoying motherhood more.

Personally, I'm loving it. The only good thing about their disappearance is that the head social worker, Ms Clinch, is letting my granddaughter, Sabrina, stay with me. I've also got custody of Damon's Range Rover and his pit bull terrier. Fortunately, the extension is now finished!

Do forward the enc's if you can.

All best wishes,

Vera

Lodge 202/203
Far Shores Trailer Park

Definitely Wednesday

Dear Irene,

Clearly you have not 'come to your senses' at all.
What on earth are you doing living rough at your age?
To say nothing of being a fugitive. Are you sure you
got the right medication off that drugs trolley at the
Clinic? It certainly doesn't sound like it.

For goodness' sake come home. You are behaving
very selfishly, which of course is the mark of an alcoholic. I'm sure Lesley is very worried about you –
when she has a moment between being a full-time
mother and a full time estate agent. I certainly am. I
wouldn't trust a dog to the care of those two. In fact,
our social worker, Ms Clinch, confided she'd been on to
the RSPCA about the pit bull terrier.

Yours,

Vera

PS Just remember, 'I am an alcoholic.'

PPS Damon *is* paranoid as a result of the medication
he's on. I don't advise you to try it.

PPPS Nearly forgot. Please give Karen the enc. from social services.

Social Services
The Old Armoury
Grimm Street
Vicker-upon-St Agnes

Tuesday 18th

Dear Ms Karen Smalls,

I write to inform you that we are awarding temporary custody of your daughter, Sabrina Smalls, to Mrs Vera Smalls, her grandmother. We have taken all factors into account, including your contention of mental abuse in your childhood – though frankly, we don't usually see 'bursting into the bathroom when I was on the lavatory' as an abuse issue.

Your recent abandonment of your child has left us no other option.

Yours sincerely

Christobel Clinch
Social worker

Kookaburra's Rest
Lirralirra Falls
Australia

Thank God it's Friday

Dear Vera,

So much has happened here since I last wrote I
hardly know where to start. I began to feel much more
clear-headed when Damon confiscated my medication
shortly after I wrote and started to take it himself.
Unfortunately he grew even odder and rather aggressive. He thought Karen was a dingo and that she had
swallowed her own baby, and kept pointing to her
pregnant belly and shouting, 'Why's she so fat then,
you tell me that?!' It was very upsetting and has made
me do a complete rethink about my stance on banning
sex education in schools. At least they could tell them
that babies come out of ladies' tummies.

Anyway, Karen and I were so frightened that I
decided to call my daughter, Lesley, to see if we could
go there for a while. Apart from anything else, I only
had the clothes I stood up in, and they were pretty
grubby to say the least. She told us where to go (see
above address), and to stay there till she arrived, which
is what we are doing. It's a lovely little guesthouse, and
it seems they know Lesley here quite well. They say
she often comes to stay here with a gentleman friend,
but I'm sure they must have got that wrong.

She also read me the letters you sent. Karen was very
angry about you getting custody of Sabrina – she said

she asked you to take care of her for a while, while she came to rescue me, so what's all the fuss about? Then she found the note that she thought she'd left you, in her handbag, so now she doesn't blame you quite as much. I hope that the two of you manage to reconcile your differences – she's all for you doing family therapy together when she returns. I know for a fact that she still has recurring nightmares about the lavatory incidents the social worker dismissed so lightly.

I think we'll stay at Lesley's for a while, just to catch our breath, and then fly home in a couple of weeks, so if you're writing, please send letters there.

All for now, love

Irene

PS I think the drugs they gave me in the clinic made me a bit forgetful. I had no idea you were an alcoholic! I'm so sorry for you. I think they say, 'One step at a time,' don't they? Please try not to give in to temptation, particularly now you have become a temporary mother to your granddaughter.

Lodge 202/203
Far Shores Trailer Park

Sunday

Dear Irene,

The drugs must have addled your brain completely if you've forgotten *you* are the alcoholic! If you imagine the occasional sweet sherry is at all the same thing then you are much mistaken. I may have had one too many at the odd occasion – a wedding or a funeral, let's say – but I have never been through a crate on my own. There is absolutely no comparison. As if I would endanger the life of my dear little daughter – I mean *grand*daughter. You may wish to tell Karen, by the way, that Sabrina is fine and doesn't miss her at all. Well, why should she? She tells me Karen used to bribe her to stay under the bed when one of her unsuitable men came round. The things that child has seen! Karen is someone to complain about lavatory incidents. It looks as though Damon follows the pattern. Perhaps, now you have had a close encounter yourself, you are more inclined to believe me.

Here, Sabrina has my undivided attention. Apart from the dog. We've just come back from a lovely walk on the beach – he's covered in seaweed! Of course we have to poop-and-scoop and stop him savaging toddlers, but he seems happier, poor thing. We paddled and skimmed stones and now we're playing on Sabrina's computer. (Yasmin got one from the cash and carry.) My favourite game is 'Helicopter GunChix'!

Lots of girls in camouflage blasting all the baddies. Sabrina says she's going to be one when she grows up. And to think I wanted to be a librarian.

Let me know if and when you are returning and I will meet you with the Range Rover. I suppose I can do no less. You *are* my best friend, and Karen *is* my daughter.

I'll keep my fingers crossed for a speedy return of your memory.

All best wishes,

Vera

Lodge 202/203
Far Shores Trailer Park

Sunday

Dear Lesley,

I can't express how sorry I am you've been landed with both Irene and Karen. Let's hope Damon doesn't turn up as well – he can be very violent. Normally it's worse when he's taking drugs, and I understand from Irene he's currently taking her tablets from the Clinic. Heaven knows what they are.

If there is anything I can do to help, short of having them back here, do let me know.

Fond regards and good luck!

Vera

St Urban
Melbourne
Australia

Dear Vera,

Here we are at Lesley's, safe and sound, so got your last, at last. I haven't told Karen any of the hurtful things you asked me to pass on, except to say that you are keeping her daughter Sabrina safe and well.

So far we've had no trouble from Damon since we escaped his clutches, although the television news is full of a 'Mystery Dingo Man' wandering around in the area of the bush where we last saw him, which could be him. If it is, he has apparently joined a pack of dingoes and is walking on all fours, and, if the artists' impressions are to be believed, has grown even more hirsute than usual.

Many things have become much clearer for me, and I have to say that your Karen has been a boon in that regard. She's explained things to me that I have obviously led too sheltered an existence to even dream of.

I think I do remember being a bit depressed, and yes – drinking a little too much – although where you get the idea I am an alcoholic I'll go to my grave never knowing. I was so very lonely. I'd travelled half-way round the world to see my daughter, and most of the time she was out. Of course it was lovely being able to be with my granddaughter, Cheryl Marie, every day, but there is only so much meaningful conversation you can have with a little girl her age. Australia is so very far away from everywhere, and I started to feel a bit stranded and hopeless, and wondering what I could possibly do to make my life better. All I could come up with was 'Nothing'. Actually, that wasn't quite all I could come up with. I also invented a nice story for myself to cheer myself up, about a man called Vincent. He did exist – still does, as far as I'm aware – but I exaggerated the depth of our relationship a little bit. In fact, our only contact was pairing each other in serve-and-volley practice on one occasion. I also gave him rather more hair and teeth in my fantasy than he actually possesses in real life. But I digress.

I remember hitting a case of wine that Lesley had bought me rather hard one night, and then realising to my horror that I was drunk and incapable and in charge of a minor – Lesley was out as usual, and as usual I was baby-sitting. I felt very ashamed of myself, not to mention extremely giddy and horribly nauseous. I put myself under a cold shower and started to feel a little more clear-headed, and then I remembered some special herbal tea I had seen Lesley taking at night-time which she keeps in a caddy in her smalls drawer. When I'd asked her what it was, she'd said it helped to calm her down and get things in perspective, so naturally I thought it might be just the thing to sober me up. I put the kettle on, and given how much I needed to get things in perspective, put two spoonfuls in for me, and three for the pot.

Vera, you'll never guess in a million years what Karen now tells me it was! Illegal drugs! Something called maryjuana – have you heard of it? According to her, I took enough of the stuff to send me right off what remained of my rocker!

Naturally I have told Lesley off now in no uncertain terms about taking drugs, although both she and Karen tell me I'm making a fuss about nothing. They say that even the Home Secretary has admitted to taking it when he was a student, although apparently he doesn't admit to inhaling. Frankly I don't know what difference that makes – I mean, who would inhale when they're drinking tea?

Anyway, she's promised me she won't do it again, so I suppose some good has come out of it. Another piece of nice news is that our daughters seem to be following in our footsteps and have become almost inseparable pals. Even now as I write they are holed up in Lesley's bedroom together having a really good girls' night in – I can hear their merry giggles from out here on the veranda! Not that I feel left out.

Well, all for now. I'm still very tired and keep needing to catch up on my sleep, but I wanted to put your mind at rest that all is as well as can be expected, and that Karen and I will be staying on here for a while longer.

Lots of love,

Irene

Lodge 202/203
Far Shores Trailer Park

Dear Irene,

Fond of you as I am, I would never describe us as
'inseparable'. In my opinion we are at our best with
several thousand miles between us. However, I am
very glad to hear you seem to have regained your wits
and can now tell the difference between herbal tea and
mind-altering substances. Incidentally, next time you
feel the need to gain perspective, or 'chill out' in trailer-
park parlance, you might try two drops of lavender oil
and a candle in the bath (Yasmin's recipe), a sheep's
yoghurt massage (my son Howard's) or Horlicks, a
hot-water bottle and a good book (mine).

I'm glad the 'girls' are getting on so well. Perhaps
Lesley (who seems so affectionate) will teach Karen
some manners. I'm a little concerned about the giggling
– are you sure you threw away the rest of the mari-
juana? In my experience of addicts (everyone in the
trailer-park, including the children), just saying 'no' is
not an option. I know for a fact that Karen and Damon
smoked home-grown 'grass', as they call it, every day.
Trust Karen. And when she's pregnant as well. The
baby will certainly have green fingers – at this rate it
will be lucky to escape a green head. Is she intending
to have it there, by the way? In which case it will be
Australian. Appropriate enough, I suppose, since its
father is a dingo.

Well, on to more pleasant topics. Sabrina and I are
planting a garden round the trailer. It's too late for it to

bloom this year, of course, but it should be lovely for the Spring. If we are still here, that is. Social Services are considering rehousing us. Ms Clinch is not happy with the company Sabrina keeps (see above) – something about 'peer pressure'. Though I must say, whatever their problems, Yasmin's children are charming. They've just been round with some seedlings for us to plant in the window boxes.

Whoops – I can see scuds of earth flying past the window. The dog is digging. We've renamed him 'Rex' after Tyrannosaurus, since, depending on how much grass he had smoked, Damon used to call him 'Ronnie' or 'Reg'. No wonder the poor thing is violent. I'd better go and rescue my poor plants!

All for now.

My love to you,

Vera

PS Please pass the enclosed letter on to Karen.

Dear Karen,

I have spoken to Ms Clinch about your family therapy idea. To be honest she doesn't hold out much hope
for us, but I am willing to try if you are. Anything, if it
will make you less rude, judgemental and unloving.
Then again, perhaps since you're having such a good
time, you will stay in Australia.

I enclose some paintings Sabrina did for you at
school. Don't be alarmed by the female figures being
stabbed and set on fire. According to her teacher, it's
healthy for Sabrina to express her 'matricidal anger'.

We both look forward to hearing about the baby.
What a pity you won't have a partner at your side.
You'd better teach Irene 'Ten Green Bottles'. Though
come to think of it, that's the last thing she should be
singing.

Your loving Mother

St Urban
Melbourne
Australia

Dear Vera,

Or should I say, Dear Granny? Glad tidings and
great joy, for unto you a grandson is born! Mother and
baby are now doing well and came back home today.
It's amazing, isn't it, the way they turf them out of
hospital so quickly nowadays, when we were cosseted
and kept in cotton wool in nursing homes for a fortnight. Karen's labour, poor thing, was as long and
gruelling as it was sudden and unexpected. According
to her calculations, it wasn't due for another two
months, but here he is, a bonny eight and a half
pounds, and apparently fully formed. The hospital
certainly seem to think he is a full-term baby. It's made
me wonder quietly to myself if Damon could be the
father. How long has she known him? It can't be nine
months already, can it?

Certainly there is no trace of Damon in his looks,
you'll be relieved to know. He has a much higher fore-
head, for a start, and what there is so far of his hair is a
beautiful golden colour. He has long legs and very
refined hands, and a look of intelligence in his eyes that
I have never noticed in Damon. Best of all, as far as
you're concerned, is that you have another grandchild
born with your very distinctive nose, so there's
certainly no mix-up as to who his grandmother is!

All for now as I'm supposed to be washing nappies.

Karen is very Eco, isn't she? She says it would take a forest the size of Sherwood to provide enough raw materials to keep him in disposables until he's potty-trained, and she has more respect for the planet than that. Just goes to show we weren't wrong about every-thing when we were young mums!

I've taken some photos of mother and son and will send them when they're developed, in my next. No name for the little chap yet, as Karen wants to get to know his personality first. She has a theory that wrong naming can cripple a child's development. Apparently she's always seen herself as being more of a Cassandra than a Karen. She would also like his lineage to be reflected in his second and third names, and asks to be reminded of the names of her two grandfathers. Can you let us know?

Congratulations, Granny Small!

More soon,

With love,

Nanny Spencer!!

Lodge 202/203
Far Shores Trailer Park

Dear Irene,

Sorry about the delay in responding. Life on the
trailer park has been even more dramatic than usual.
Yasmin was hard up, so she dumped her kids with me
and went to Amsterdam for a few days. Apparently
they are very keen on her massages over there and give
her a lovely little booth with curtains and a pink light,
which she says is marvellous for relaxation. She
returned to find her trailer had been completely
ransacked! Everything had gone, including her stock of
essential oils, which was disastrous as she'd completely
run out – she'd had such a busy time with them. We
didn't hear a thing, but of course one gets used to the
nightly screams, shouts and crashes. Once my sponge
earplugs are in I could sleep through a chainsaw
massacre! The police have refused to investigate, as the
park is a 'no-go' area, but Site Security, who are always
informed when people go away, say that there has been
a spate of raids and we're the victims of a serial
ransacker. I must talk to Dave-next-door-but-one about
getting iron bars for the windows.

Naturally we are delighted that Karen has been
safely delivered. I'm not surprised her labour took so
long. After breaking my waters two weeks early at a
Masonic dinner dance, she took the rest of the fortnight
to arrive. By the time she was born I was crawling
round the floor begging to be put out of my misery.

The father of the new baby is as much a mystery to me as it probably is to her. I have no idea what she got up to before she met Damon. Sabrina remembers a tall blond man who visited Howard at Sheepdipper's. She thinks he was the vet. I didn't like to probe – she's only six – but she says he and Karen often went to the sheep shed together. Someone has to hold the sheep's head while the vet shoves his hand up the other end, so perhaps one thing led to another. But I'd be amazed if it's any friend of Howard's – as far as I know, they are all of the 'other persuasion'.

Please give Karen the enclosed card and baby-grow. I got one with the longest legs, so I hope it will accommodate. Sabrina is really looking forward to seeing the pictures of her little brother. As to names, Karen's paternal grandfather was called Wilfred, but he was rather unpleasant. Karen never liked sitting on his knee. My father was a Charlie. Sabrina suggests 'Robbie', after her favourite pop star.

Must finish and cook tea for all the kids and Yasmin. I'm feeding them until Yasmin gets a new cooker installed. It's a good job she did so well in Amsterdam. She insists she loves her work, but I must say she looks knackered.

Love to you all and a kiss for my new grandson. It's getting to be quite a tribe!

Vera

PS It appears I *did* sleep through a chainsaw massacre. Security tell me there was one the other night at Trailer

206. A 'domestic' that got out of hand. The trailer's just a pile of splintered wood and there were no survivors.

St Urban
Melbourne
Australia

Dear Vera,

Here at last are the photographs of 'Baby Boy Small'
– still no name yet, so we're calling him by the name
that was on his hospital armband. Makes him sound
like a boxer, doesn't it?! Sorry the pictures are a bit
blurred, but I was trembling with nerves trying to use
the new camera I'd treated myself to. It says it's fully
automatic on the box, and then when you get it home
you find it's like a computer, full of digital whatsits
and 'menus', whatever they are. So far I haven't found
anything on one that you would want to eat. Anyway,
as you see, I had to put it on the 'Panamaric Menu' so
we could get the full length of his legs in. Isn't he
bonny?! I'm glad at least that his nose is in focus, so
you can see for yourself how it runs in the family.

I am so sorry to hear of the level of violence and civil
unrest at Far Shores Trailer Park. No wonder your
social worker Ms Clinch wants to get you moved. Any
joy yet? When I mentioned it to Karen she gave what
we used to call an 'old-fashioned look', and recom-
mends that you don't ever tell Site Security when
you're going away. She says that when Damon was
working for them they used to take it as a *carte blanche*
for going in and helping themselves to people's possessions. She also said that if you look inside the Range
Rover's inner mysteries, you will see that something
called the 'shassy' number has been filed off. Of course,

it could just be a filament of her over-active imagination, but maybe you'd better check – you could be found guilty of driving stolen goods. Perhaps Dave-next-door-but-one could help you identify the 'shassy' – I'm afraid I've no idea what one is.

Karen is doing well *'post partum'*, and in fact has expressed some of her milk so that I can feed Baby Boy tonight while she and Lesley go for a 'girls' night out'. I must say she's recovered her figure quickly, judging by her costume choice when they left!

Anyway, mustn't luxuriate too long in the world of words – Nanny Spencer is on full time duty tonight! Plus I am having to run myself up a few frocks since apparently Lesley mistakenly sent all my clothes back to England. Could you send me that Butterick pattern you used to have for the box-pleated summer frock, if you still have it to hand? I know it's old, but it always looked so timeless on you.

Baby Boy sends a kiss to his Granny Small and to his sister Sabrina.

Love,

Irene

Lodge 202/203
Far Shores Trailer Park

Dear Irene,

Thank you for your newsy letter and the photos of
the baby. Or rather, his nose. It looks like a trunk. I can
see no resemblance to mine at all. And those legs
certainly don't come from my side of the family. Baby
Boy 'Small' seems most inappropriate. Sabrina was
terribly disappointed – she of course is so petite and her
nose is a little button – much more like Granny's. We
both think it's time he had a proper name, whatever
nonsense Karen spouts about his 'personality'. At this
rate he will grow up without one. Sabrina took another
look at the pictures and suggested 'Gubby' after her
goldfish. Though to be honest, 'Gummy' would be
nearer the mark. I hope you've mastered the camera by
the next set. Are you sure the shaking hands were due
to nerves, and not one too many 'you-know-whats'? I'm
sorry if that sounds blunt but, as a true friend, I
consider it my duty to be vigilant.

I *do* know what you mean about technology. Yasmin
has finally got her new digi-cooker installed and I have
been trying to use it. (Yasmin, poor love, has had to
take a night job.) It's got hundreds of labour-saving
devices, but a 'menu' – which in the case of a cooker
you might expect – is the last thing I can find. I can't
even get the blasted gas to light. The children have had
to have sandwiches for the last few days. I've telephoned British Gas a dozen times, but all I get is
Vivaldi. That poor man must be turning in his grave at

what they've done to his 'Four Seasons'!

I've also had to forbid Sabrina access to the 'net'. She kept trying to download pornography. It's the influence of Yasmin's kids, I'm afraid. They whizz about all over the place on it. Sometimes it's hard to tell if they're playing violent techno-games or watching worldwide atrocities. Speaking of which, Ms Clinch brought some charming refugees to view the trailer. They liked it much better than the converted lavatory they'd been camping in and weren't a bit put off by the murder and mayhem on the site. They said they'd been living with that for years in Kosovo. I'm keeping my fingers crossed, though the trailer, even with extension, is a little small for ten of them.

Must stop – it's time to wrestle with the cooker again. Where will it all end? Trust men to do away with God and put a microchip in his place. It will serve them right if everything does collapse on 1st Jan. 2000! I suppose we women, as usual, will have to pick up the pieces. And make the sandwiches.

My love as ever,

Vee

PS Almost forgot. Looked everywhere for that Butterick pattern, but no joy. I threw masses away when I moved here – as I'm sure I've mentioned, space is limited. I'm sending the frock instead. I haven't worn it for years. I'm sure you can let it out in the right places.

PPS Dave-next-door-but-one is in bed with his back, so

I asked Terry-who-makes-the-sex-videos about the 'shassy'. He laughed and said the only one he'd ever laid a finger on was Carol's. Given the nature of their 'work', I didn't inquire further.

St Urban
Australia

Dear Vera,

Thank you for the frock, which I've managed to take in after battling for long hours with the thirty-six box pleats. In order to get it to fit me (being petite) I've had to reduce it to twenty-four pleats while letting out the bust a little. Quite a job! In fact I'd have been quicker if I'd woven the material myself before making it! However, since it was so voluminous in the skirt, I had enough material left over to make a little frock for Cheryl Marie and a tiny little top for Baby Boy. You can imagine, we cut quite a dash when we go shopping together in them, which we did today. One old lady with whom we queued for vegetables at the market said we reminded her of the Beverley Sisters! I haven't thought of them for years, have you? They were so wonderful, and such beautiful '*chanteuses*', and such a nice picture of 'family', don't you think? It's such a pity that the young don't have such clean-cut, normal, effer-vacious role models any more, isn't it? It's no wonder Yasmin's children run a bit wild when the pop heroes are called things like 'Beastie Boys' these days. If only Sir Cliff Richard was still top of the pops – it would be such a different story.

Which brings me to your good deeds. Vera, are you sure you aren't biting off more than you can chew by offering a home to those refugees? It is so kind of you, but surely, when you had the extension built, it was so that you and Sabrina had more room for yourselves, not so you could become another branch of the Red Cross? Where on earth will you all sleep? Surely you are already doing enough for the community by feeding a prostitute's children? Which of course is very Christian of you, but then again it would be, wouldn't it? Jesus himself was our generation's role model. In fact if it hadn't been for Sunday School and lessons about Mary Magdalene, I probably would still be none the wiser about 'the oldest profession'.

It is the weekend here – well, come to think of it, I suppose it is the weekend there, but when you're so far away it's difficult to imagine things happening at the same time – and Lesley has taken Karen away to Kookaburra's Rest to 'chill out', which I believe is what they say these days instead of 'to relax'. Kookaburra's Rest, upstate in Lirralirra, was where we stayed, you may remember, when we ran away from Damon after he had decided he was a dingo. There has been some dramatic and tragic news of him, which is why Karen needs to be 'chilled out' – newspaper cutting enc. She is debating whether to help police with their inquiries, but I think she will prefer to keep silent. She doesn't want Baby Boy to be tainted with a lurid past by the gutter press, and I can't say I blame her.

Anyway, mustn't stop. Nappies to wash, entertainment for Cheryl Marie to be organised, babies to be bathed! The fridge is full to bursting with expressed milk – Karen said she felt like a Friesian cow before she left! I feel as if I could do with 'chilling out' myself, to be absolutely honest!

Take care, and do think about what I said about giving too much to others.

With love,

Irene

PS Just a thought – apropos of Yasmin's digi-cooker – could it be possible that you can't light the gas because it's electric?

PPS 'A slab of tinnies' is a case of lager, I believe, and a chook is a chicken – see news cutting.

The Daily Digger

'I SAVED AUSTRALIA FROM THE DINGO MAN AND NOW I'M BEING PUNISHED!'

An Eyewitness Account as told to *Digger* Reporter
Stu Jackson

PETE DALEWOOD is a good bloke. Everybody what knows him says so. And so's his wife Bev. They don't lie, they can handle a couple of slabs of tinnies apiece, and both of them are bloody good shots. A perfect pair of Ockers, you might say, but that's where you'd be wrong, according to whingeing sissy liberal police chief Franco Bianchi.

A dab hand with the rifle, and a keen reader of our sister magazine *Gotcha!*, Pete was shooting a few dingo vermin while posing for Bev's amature photos what they hoped would get printed in 'Readers' Pickies' in the mag next month. Bang! Crack! Bull's-eye! Another dingo falls to Pete's top gun!! But when they stroll over to inspect the shot patterns, instead of a dingo there's a hairy bloke turned belly up, dead as a doornail and ten times as bloody.

'Bev and me was minding our own business,' says Pete today from his police cell, 'taking a few shots at some dingoes what were killing our chooks. What's a bloke supposed to do, for Christ's sake? Let 'em eat your chooks and turn the other cheek? How was I supposed to know at that distance that one of em was a human being? 'Sides, everybody knows that Dingo Man's been terrorising the whole of Australia. If I had him in my sights right now, I'd do the same thing again. What's happen-

ing to this bloody country? In other places in the world, I'd be a hero, not a crim.'

Now we can all sleep safe in our beds at night, Pete is being charged with murder, and the little lady is grieving at home alone. 'It's that bloody poofter anti-gun lobby,' says Bev, a blonde beauty. 'They've got that wog Bianchi by the short and curlies. Pete done good, and look where it got him. I'm starting a campaign, and anybody what wants to join up can turn up at the demo tomorrow. I am standing by my man. He's a hero. That Dingo Man is now where he belongs – in hell. And I know a few other people what ought to be joining him!'

The Dingo Man's identity is still a mystery, but as readers will see from Bev's superb close-ups on pages 3 and 4, the tattoos 'Rule Britannia' and 'Arsenal for Ever' tell their own tale. 'If Poms want to come here and get back to nature,' says Pete, 'that's their business. But now they know what happens to 'em if they do.'

*Vera and Sabrina and Rex have moved
to a new home!*

New Address:

**Flat 2
19-23 Mandela Court
Thrush Grove
Vicker-upon-St Agnes**

Dear Irene,

No room on this postcard for more than a quick
hello! Ms Clinch came up trumps. Apart from some
strange fungicidal growth in the crevices, this s/c, two
bdrm, all elec., digi-free council flt with pkg and gdn is
delightful. I must say it's a relief to be off the trailer
park. The chainsaw incident was the last straw – or
perhaps I should say 'splinter'. I do hope the refugees
will be all right there. I understand they are Muslim, so
I left them the mats and a rack full of vegetables. I
drew the line at Halal chicken, though I'm sure the
chainsaw wielder would have obliged.

More as soon as we are settled,

Vee

PS Am writing to Howard to try to find out if Baby
Boy's possible father, the vet, is still around.

Flat 2
19–23 Mandela Court
Thrush Grove
Vicker-upon-St Agnes

Dear Howard,

A quick note with my new address. The council finally rehoused us. You may like to know, as I'm sure Karen won't have informed you, that you now have a large Australian nephew known as 'Baby Boy Small'. His father – as far as we know – has been shot dead whilst masquerading as a dingo (it's a long story – don't ask), so he, like Sabrina, will grow up without one. Perhaps, under the circumstances, that is a blessing. I don't think a dingo is the best role model. Do you, by any chance, still have that nice vet? You might like to mention Karen's news to him.

Will stop now. Busy with decorating. When we arrived everything was red, green and gold!

Mumsie

St Urban
Melbourne
Australia

Dear Vee and Sabrina,

Welcome to your new home! I am delighted to hear
you have escaped the trailer park, and wish you
certain happiness and peace in Mandela Court. You
may be surprised to know that its good influence has
already made its mark 'Down Under' – when I
showed your postcard to Karen and she saw your new
address, she was inspired to finally name Baby Boy. A
big welcome then, please, for Nelson Wilfred Charlie
St John Small! (The first two middle names are for his
great-grandparents, of course, but I don't know who
is responsible for the 'St John' part, and when I asked
Karen, she and Lesley only smirked and giggled
together. I tried to pump Lesley for information when
I got her on her own, but she pretended not to know
what I was talking about. They are as thick as thieves
these days, our daughters. Not that I feel left out.
Anyway, it might be something else to quiz Howard
about, re the vet's name.)

Must stop now, as I've been asked to take Cheryl
Marie and little Nelson out for a walk so that Lesley
and Karen can sleep late, undisturbed. They went
'clubbing' last night, which apparently is less violent
than it sounds. We used to call it 'going to a dance'.
Their dances these days, though, don't seem to start
until midnight, and go on until breakfast time. Thank
heavens it hasn't always been like that – just think, if it

had been, Cinderella would have turned into a pump-kin while still queuing to get into the ball, and Prince Charming wouldn't have looked twice. Unless he was a devout vegetarian, I suppose.

Oh dear, I am waxing lyrical. I've been missing my creative writing classes, and really must find time to go again. Perhaps I shall pen a poem in the park while I watch over my two little charges. Watch this space!!!

Much love,

Irene

Flat 2
19–23 Mandela Court
Thrush Grove
Vicker-upon-St Agnes

Dear 'Nanny Spencer',

Thank you for the lovely card. Sabrina has pinned it
to her wall. Her bedroom is still red, green and gold,
which she tells me are 'roots'. I don't know what she
means – I've never seen a parsnip in those colours.

We send love, and some new clothes, for Nelson and
Cheryl Marie. I'd like them to wear something from
me, other than a made-over box pleat. The dungarees
can be let down if Nelson continues to elongate. Aren't
the baby trainers sweet? They are thirty pounds in the
shops here, but Yasmin gets them by the caseload from
one of her clients who is a footwear specialist. She lays
her hands on all sorts of things since she has taken her
night job.

You are certainly whole-heartedly embracing your
role of head cook and nappy washer. It sounds to me
as though your goodwill is being rather exploited. I
can't speak for Lesley, but Karen is, and always will
be, a taker. She can wind people round her little finger
– or in some cases, other parts of her anatomy.
Presumably that's why it's on display when she goes
'clubbing'. In no time she'll be in another unsuitable
liaison and – perish the thought – another type of
'club'. I hope she doesn't suppose she is going to walk
into this flat, or indeed any other council accommodation, when she returns with Nelson. Tony Blair is very

down on single mothers. Especially serial ones. I imagine she will be a candidate for compulsory sterilisation.

Do take up your writing again. Creative or not, you must have something to while away the long hours on your own. Of course you have the children, and I adore Sabrina, but there are times when I long for a grown-up conversation – classical music, Art, double glazing . . .

We have finished painting the rest of Mandela Court. It is now a tasteful terracotta and very peaceful – apart from the African drumming. There! No sooner do I mention it than it starts again! Must go and investigate . . .

Later:
Sabrina and I had the most marvellous evening in No. 4, learning the female courting rituals of the Astarte tribe. Sara, my neighbour, is a Princess from it. The drum rhythms are compulsive. Everyone, from kids to pensioners, was gyrating madly. Apparently, in Africa, age is no handicap. Felt like a girl again! I could teach Karen and Lesley something about dancing. And courting. Next week we are having a session with the male members.

Must finish. Exhausted.

A bosom bounce and a hip wobble,

Vee

Flat 2
19–23 Mandela Court
Thrush Grove
Vicker-upon-St Agnes

Dear Howard,

Karen has given your nephew a string of names
longer than royalty. For everyday purposes, he will be
known as 'Nelson'. I suppose a christening is out of the
question, but do drop her a line.

Just remind me, was that nice vet called St John?

Mumsie xx

St Urban
Melbourne
Australia

Dear Vera,

In Deepest Sympathy
✝

Excuse the inappropriate card – it was all I had in
my stationery box until I can find time to go out to the
shops again, and I've used up all my notepaper in the
penning of poems – one enc. for your perusal – thanks
for encouraging me back to so pleasant a pastime.
Lesley and Karen have gone up to Queensland for a
week to lie down on the beach. Not that I feel left out.
They are both suffering from exhaustion, apparently.

A big 'thank-you' from Cheryl Marie and Nelson for
their new clothes. Yes, the pair of baby 'trainers' are
very sweet, and after a good scrubbing I was able to
clean off the rather nasty staining that was inside the
left one. As you'll see from the enc. photos, Nelson has
already grown in length since you last saw his picture,
so until I find time to let his dungarees down, he is
wearing them at the fashionable 'pedal-pusher' length.

More soon. Any news from Howard about the vet?

Much love from your poet pal,

Irene

PS Are 'blue bags' still available in England, do you know? Even when I boil them, the nappies are coming out a rather beige colour, which would certainly never have got past my mother's high standards. If you find any, please send them and I will reimburse.

Britannia – An Ode

by
Irene Spencer

O England,
You are so far away.
I wish that I could visit you,
If only for a day.

But I am needed here, my dear,
To watch o'er two of your babes.
To keep them safe and sound for you
Across the briny waves.

If I was there (or you were here),
I'd worship at your feet.
I'd wave at smiling bobbies and
I'd keep my garden neat.

I'd polish my silver tea set,
I'd wolf my fish and chips,
Your name, and praise accordingly,
Would never be off my lips.

O England,
You are the best there is,
How could I have forgot?
But I am here, and you are there,
And my heart aches quite a lot.

Flat 2
19–23 Mandela Court
Thrush Grove
Vicker-upon-St Agnes

Dear Irene,

I'm really worried about you. Perhaps it is 'Poetic Licence', but you are euphemising an England which hasn't existed since the 1950s! It's clear you are very homesick. By the way, I've looked everywhere for Dolly Blues, as they used to be called, but like so much else, they haven't survived the onslaught of 'modernisation'. Are you, perhaps, feeding Nelson too much spinach? I recall my mother used to complain about the colour of tripe, which, as cows eat grass, was, in its natural state, green. I believe she used to soak it in bleach before putting it on my father's plate with gravy and onions. I don't think she ever used Dolly Blue. But that, as I was saying, was in the old days. I haven't seen tripe for sale for years. Makes one wonder, with all these new-fangled farming methods, whether cows still have stomachs.

I've spent sleepless hours (to be honest, not too many – I've been happily buggered after the African dance classes) thinking of you penning your verses in the lonely night. I'm sure with two children to look after, you don't get the time, except in the wee small hours. Be wary – that's the time temptation strikes. We don't want you back in the funny farm.

Surely it's you who should be taking the holiday? Why don't you come home for one? You are welcome to stay here and share the joys of Mandela Court. We now have lots of African carvings and rugs and some wonderfully erotic tropical plants (the central heating is *very* effective). I can put Sabrina on the African reed 'futon' and you can have her room – as long as the colours don't bring on your migraine. It will only be for a short time, of course – I realise you are indispensable in St Urban.

Do reply soon, dear. Preferably not in the ode form.

All our love,

Vee and Sabrina

PS Are you allergic to dogs?

Sheepdipper's Shed
Shooters Hill
Shale, Shap
Nr Great Shagthorne

Darling Mumsie,

It's funny you should mention St John. *He's* been asking about the family. Well, about Karen to be specific. Waxing lyrical about their shared moments over entrails, in the sheep shed. Told the dear boy about the new addition and he got quite excited. Says he can't wait to see Nelson. I've sent Karen a gorgeous baby boiler-suit that Antony made out of sheepskin, and I've asked her for some photographs.

Is she coming home? Antony would adore a baby – you know how broody he gets. Besides, we miss Karen for the milking (the sheep, I mean!).

Your loving son,

Howie

St Urban
Melbourne
Australia

Dear Vee,

You will *never* guess what's happened now, never
ever in a million years. I'm reeling from the shock. I
know I've been busy, but I can't believe I've been so
blind! Lesley is marrying her boss!!!! Or at least, she
intends to, once he's got a divorce from the very angry
lady who called round to see me while Lesley and
Karen were in Queensland. It turns out my daughter
has been having an affair with the lady's husband for a
year! Apparently 'Brian' – for that is his nomenclature –
was in Queensland with them – his wife had him
followed by a private detective.

You may think this shocking enough, but there's
more. When Lesley got back from her holiday, I
confronted her with my new and terrible knowledge,
and begged her, in the name of decency, to leave the
poor woman's husband alone. 'No, Mum,' she says, as
bold as brass, 'it's too late for that.' When I continued
to press my point, she suddenly got very angry and
pointed at her stomach, and screamed 'I'm up the
spout, you blind old bat, and it's his!' Vee – I'm going
to be a granny again, in five months' time! Then, without another word, she and Karen went out 'clubbing' –
they said Lesley needed to taste her freedom as much
as possible before she was 'lumbered' again with
another baby.

Vera, I hope you are sitting down, because there's

even more. No sooner had I sat down with a small sherry to digest this news than there was a knock at the door, and when I went to answer it, a blonde man with a suitcase and extraordinarily long legs bounced into the house and dashed past me, shouting, 'Where is he? Where's my baby boy?' Naturally, thinking this was 'Brian', and knowing now from the Damon experience that a lot of men are very naive about making babies, I told him it was still in Lesley's tummy, where it would be staying for some long time yet, and he'd just have to wait. I knew I'd made a mistake when he asked me who the hell Lesley was, but I'd no idea how much of a mistake until he suddenly pulled himself together, apologised very nicely, said he was sorry then, perhaps he'd got the wrong house – he was looking for a Karen and Nelson Small – it was St John the Vet, come all the way from Great Shagthorne!!

As I write, in the wee small hours, Lesley is canoodling in her bedroom with 'Brian', Karen is curled up with St John in what used to be my room, and I am folded up on the sofa in the nursery with Cheryl Marie and Nelson. Not that I feel left out.

Heaven knows what tomorrow will bring! I'm wrung out and exhausted. If this is 'modernisation'and a taste of the new Minellium, please show me the way back to the 1950s immediately, Dolly Blues, bleached tripe and all! I'm too distressed even to write a poem.

Yours, shocked to the core,

Irene

PS I said a *small* sherry, Vera, just in case you're about to make silly and wild accusations again. Just remember – you're the one who said 'I am an alcoholic', not me.

Sheepdipper's Shed
Shooters Hill
Shale, Shap
Nr Great Shagthorne

Dearest darling Mumsie,

It's Horrorsville here – total chaos. St John, the vet, just took off in the middle of the insemination season, saying his own offspring was more important. If you ask me, he's been a bit too free with his services. The sheep are wandering around, bleating madly. So is Antony. He can't manage to impregnate them on his own, and he knows I faint at the sight of a syringe. He gets terribly cross with me, but, as I say, at least it ensures I'll never become a drug addict.

You absolutely must persuade them to come back. St John is indispensable, even if he is usually out of it on animal tranqs. That's why we're so late with the sheep – it took us months to drag him from his hovel. But he's the only vet we'll ever get around here. We'll even put up with Karen for his sake. And of course, we'd welcome the baby. There's a pair of fabby sheep-skin boots waiting, and Antony's already started casting the Runes for his future. He definitely sees him as a 'sheep' person, though I've pointed out he isn't an Aries – thank goodness.

Please, please, do what you can. They can't be meaning to bring Nelson up with that frightful accent!

Your loving son,

Howie

Flat 2
19–23 Mandela Court
Thrush Grove
Vicker-upon-St Agnes

My dear Irene,

It never rains but it pours! Both of our daughters
with new men and new babies! Let's hope it's wedding
bells all round – and I don't care if that does make me
sound old-fashioned!

You must come home immediately. Bring Cheryl
Marie if necessary. I doubt Lesley will mind. Brian
certainly won't. In my experience, men are a bit odd
about adopting other males' children. There's plenty of
room at Mandela Court. And I can assure you, you
won't feel left out. This is a thriving, multi-national
community – even Australians are welcome.

What are Karen's and St John's plans, do you know?
I'm sure Lesley will want her 'space' back, now she has
'Brian'. No matter how bonded she and Karen have
become, men always take precedence over female
friendship. Please convey my good wishes to Karen
and St John, and tell them that there's a home for their
new family-to-be in Great Shagthorne.

Let me know your thoughts, and meanwhile I'll have
a word with the social worker, Ms Clinch, about hous-
ing. I'm sure our granddaughters would get on like a
house on fire – not one of Ms Clinch's, of course! They
are of an age, after all. It would give us a little respite
too. Much as I love her, Sabrina runs me off my feet – I
never expected to be looking after a small child again

at my age. If I complain to my new neighbour, Princess Sara of the Astarte, she just laughs. She has six children and twenty-four grandchildren. They are in and out of her flat all the time. I've no idea how many actually live there.

You would love our jolly, neighbourly evenings – photos enc. That's me in the African turban. Will finish, as I must go and sweep up the beer cans in the court. We have a Residents' Rota, but it seems to fall mostly to Sara and me. We have to keep a clean front, in case of an unexpected raid by 'Environmental'. At least you wouldn't be drinking alone if you moved here. And whatever you say, one 'small' sherry tends to lead to another.

Write soon,

All our love,

Vee

St Urban
Melbourne
Australia

Dear Vera,

Naturally we in St Urban are so relieved that you have taken time out of your busy schedule of going to neighbouring royalty's parties and clearing up your empty beer cans, to find time to organise all our lives, including where we will live and with whom.

Let me tell you that my initial reaction was 'How dare she?!!!' and, 'Who does she think she is?!!!', but after sitting for some quiet reflection in the Botanical Garden I have managed to get some perspective (without recourse to maryjuana tea, I might add, before you start thinking of referring me to Drugs Counselling) and tried to see it from your point of view, distorted and erroniatious as that might be.

Obviously, as you mention it in every letter now, you have a drink problem, and this you must admit to before you will make any headway at all with combating your desire to be needed and to be in control of everything and everyone, even those of us on the other side of the world. Think about it – if one small sherry leads to another for you, then you must stop having the small sherry. It may be hard at first, but you know it makes sense.

Gradually, as the alcohol fumes clear from your brain, you will start remembering important things, like the fact that I have my own perfectly lovely home to go to back in England, at 42 The Limes, Hethergreen.

Have you forgotten so soon that you stayed with me there on the occasion of Bill Snapes's funeral (our ex-lover, if you're having trouble remembering)? But then again, I expect you have, since you were so drunk and incapable at the wake afterwards that you fell on to his widow's floral arrangements and a male member of the funeral party. Similarly, you have obviously also forgotten that the reason I left my beautiful home so suddenly to visit Australia in the first place was that you had sent Damon over to assassinate me and to destroy my flower beds.

The next revelation you might have is that Sabrina is your daughter Karen's child, not yours, and that she has left her with you to look after her until her return, which is imminent. After that, it might just dawn on you that St John, being a successful veterinarian surgeon, has his own wonderful house with grounds in neighbouring Little Shagthorne, so he does not need to be found digs in Great Shagthorne, presumably with your son Howard. You can't, of course, be expected to know that he has done Karen the honour of asking for her hand in marriage, and that she has accepted – invitation enc. They have asked me to mastermind the catering at the reception, which challenge I shall be delighted to rise to, and with which, if you care to, you are most welcome to assist.

Karen, St John, Nelson and myself are all flying back to England in a few days. I will not be kidnapping little Cheryl Marie, as her place is with her mother and Brian – who, incidentally, is besotted with her, and who can't wait to adopt her, as soon as his divorce comes through and he is free to marry again, since his previous marriage was unhappily childless. In the meantime, he will move in with Lesley to take care of her and his unborn child, as is proper in these modern circumstances.

The next time you hear from me I will be in England, by which time, I hope, you will be feeling better. It will be a relief for you to know that Karen will be moving in with St John immediately on their arrival, and will be taking little Sabrina to live with them, so you will soon have that respite from child-care duties that you were longing for in your last.

All good wishes for your speedy return to 'normal', whatever you remember that as being.

Irene

Flat 2
19–23 Mandela Court
Thrush Grove
Vicker-upon-St Agnes

Irene,

Since you have opted to completely – and in my opinion, wilfully – misunderstand the helpful suggestions I made, with only goodwill and loving friendship in mind, I have decided that all future communication will be through my solicitor. You will be hearing from her shortly. I am considering filing charges against you in a civil court for slander and intentional theft of my daughter Karen's affections. I don't imagine, with your recent record of crazed behaviour, you will have a leg to stand on. Not that you do often anyway, what with your alcohol problem.

I have also informed our social worker, Ms Clinch, of Karen's intentions towards Sabrina, and all I can say is if her frowns and expletives are anything to go by, it will be over her dead body. Social services do not look kindly on women who abandon their children, particularly if they wish to reinstall them in unsuitable accommodation. You may like to know, as indeed might Karen, that according to my son Howard, St John's 'wonderful house with grounds' consists of a bothy surrounded by a nettle patch, and that he narrowly escaped being struck off the veterinary register for over-use of animal tranquillisers. I don't give a crying baby much of a chance in that household!

As for you, you will find yourself once again in your

pokey flat, home alone, except for a bottle. I wish I could say I sympathised – it is awful to feel left out – but I'm afraid that's what you get for meddling.

Sabrina and I will be unable to attend Karen's nuptuals (invitation returned), as the date clashes with our Mandela Millennial Carnival. Sabrina is playing a steel drum on the float. As I have pointed out more than once, it is important for her to be in touch with her 'roots'. Ms Clinch is in full agreement.

Yours faithfully,

V. Small

PS Since you say you are returning within days, I shall send this to your English address to welcome you.

Ingot & Camel-Hyman (Solicitors)
Lion House
Palm Walk
Vicker-upon-St Agnes

Dear Mrs Spencer,

I have been instructed by my client, Mrs Vera Small, to inform you that she is considering legal action against you on two counts:

1. Slander: With no evidence whatsoever, you have repeatedly called her an alcoholic.

2. Malicious alienation of her daughter Karen's affections: Mrs Small has not heard from her daughter once in the many months she has been away, and nor has her granddaughter, Sabrina. Even an invitation to her impending wedding came second-hand.

Out of common decency, Mrs Small also asks me to warn you that you will find yourself out of pocket if you decide to cater the reception. She has no intention of paying, and her son, Howard, insists Ms Small's intended husband is virtually bankrupt.

We look forward to receiving your comments.

Yours sincerely,

Agabatha Adebayou (LLB, Queen of the Astarte)

42 The Limes
Hethergreen

Dear Vera,

Thank you for the warm welcome home from you
and your 'solicitor'. You both may be distressed to
know that, instead of panicking at the threats of legal
action against me, I undertook some research via the
telephone and through my local library. I feel strongly
that I must inform you that:

1. Astarte was a fertility goddess worshipped by
   the Phoenicians, and not an African tribe at all.

2. The Law Society have never heard of Agabatha
   Adebayou, and neither does she have a degree
   in law.

3. She is a member of the Ladies League of
   Basketball in Vicker-upon-St Agnes, hence the
   letters 'LLB.' after her name.

I do hope you have not paid her fees, as she is
absolutely bogus from start to finish. I showed your
letter to Karen and St John, and they laughed and
laughed. Apparently St John named his twelve-
bedroom Georgian hunting lodge 'The Bothy' as a joke,
which your humourless son, Howard, obviously didn't
get – and why should he, since he has never been
invited over? As for the animal tranquillisers, once,
while wrestling with one of Howard and Antony's

more aggressive rams, St John accidentally jabbed his own arm rather than the creature's bottom, inadvertently sedating himself for several hours.

Since you are so obviously upset about not being able to attend their wedding due to a prior engagement, Karen has moved the date forward to January 2000. She will be hand-delivering the invitation, I believe, at which point she will also be inviting you to live with them in the granny flat at 'The Bothy', so that you don't have to feel you are losing Sabrina.

All for now, as I must away to an emergency meeting of the Hethergreen Village Minellium Bus Shelter Fund Committee. I left them with a few simple chores while I was away in Australia and they have done nothing. With only a few weeks to go to the great event of the new Minellium, and nothing in Hethergreen so far to show for it, I have organised a Do-It-Ourselves Digging of the Foundations Event this morning.

I do hope this letter finds you feeling more like your old self. If so, let's start planning the menu for the New Year wedding. If not, please do not trouble yourself to reply.

Yours in memory of a long and trusty friendship,

Irene

The Coach House Apartment
The Bothy
Long Lane (you're telling me!)
Little Shagthorne

Dear Irene,

Well, here I am ensconned in the 'Granny' flat (though
St John always jokes I look much too young to be one –
what a tease that boy is!), and I must say they have
bent over backwards to make it nice for me. St John, of
course, is just a naturally kind and delightful person –
as well as rich and good-looking. Quite the Prince
Charming.

Karen, for once, seems to know how lucky she is
(especially with feet her size), and is a completely
changed person. She came to see me in Mandela Court
of her own devolition and said, 'Mum, if only I'd
realised years ago how much you needed and wanted
my love, everything would have been quite different.' I
was taken aback, I can tell you, particularly as it was a
Voodoo evening and I had white paint and feathers all
over my head and was up to my elbows in chicken
blood.

I told Sara about your suspicions, by the way, and
she roared with laughter. Agabatha, her niece, is study-
ing law at night school, and it was only silly me
supposing 'Astarte' was African. In fact, Sara is a
modern-day reincarnation of the Goddess, and the
'tribe' part are the others involved with her rites. I do
miss them.

But it's lovely to have my family close, and I shall

soon get used to seeing nothing but hills outside my window. Pushing Nelson's pram up them is the very devil!

Now, about the wedding. What do you think about 'Coq o' Vin' as the main course? (It's one of Sara's recipes.)

Vee

42 The Limes
Hethergreen

Dear Vera,

Brief note, haven't got long – the male members of
the Committee put the Minellium Bus Shelter up last
night, and it is down again this morning with the
winds. I thought at the time as I watched them doing
all that 'bonding' business with their cans of lager that
men are so fond of, hours before the concrete mixer
had even arrived, that if a thing is worth doing, it's
worth doing yourself. I really don't know why I don't
listen to myself more.

Glad you're happy being Mother-in-Law (pre-
marriage) to Prince Charming, and that you have seen
enough sense to be rescued from that cult – they are
dangerous things. It starts all jolly and fun with feathers and white paint, and ends with poison in your
orange juice and mass suicide pacts – I saw a documen-
tary on television once, and believe you me it wasn't
for the squeamish.

Now as to the wedding menu. I have been planning a
Fork and Finger, not a sit-down do, so Coq o' Vin
would be quite inappropriate. I thought you could
make your old favourite, the Blue Cheese Quiche, but
with one refinement – I've been experimenting with the
addition of chives, and it lifts it from the ordinary to the
sublime. I think we should give your salmon mousse a
miss though, given my upset tummy last time I had it at
yours, but perhaps you could mastermind the salads?

So glad we are friends again. Let me know your thoughts on the above.

Much love,

Irene

PS. I think, all things considered, it would be wise to let St John do the tasting and ordering of the wine.

The Coach House Apartment
The Bothy
Long Lane
Little Shagthorne

Dear Irene,

You certainly should listen to yourself more. Of all the rude, ungrateful, ignorant, bossy, self-opinionated, interfering . . . I could go on, but I haven't got a dictionary to hand. You'd better hold your tongue, or you'll find one of your 'Minellium' Committee putting poison in *your* orange juice. At the moment I'd be glad to supply it!

Later.
Have just been for a stiff walk up a mountain. Spoke to Jesus at the top and feel a lot better. If he could turn the other cheek for 2,000 years, I can manage till after the wedding – salad recipes enclosed.

Irene, do let's enter the Millenium as we mean to go on – with tolerance.

In love and friendship,

Vera